Managing Chronic Pain

Managing Chronic Pain

A COGNITIVE-BEHAVIORAL THERAPY APPROACH

Therapist Guide

John D. Otis

OXFORD

UNIVERSITY PRESS

2007

OXFORD
UNIVERSITY PRESS

Oxford University Press, Inc., publishes works that further
Oxford University's objective of excellence
in research, scholarship, and education.

Oxford   New York
Auckland   Cape Town   Dar es Salaam   Hong Kong   Karachi
Kuala Lumpur   Madrid   Melbourne   Mexico City   Nairobi
New Delhi   Shanghai   Taipei   Toronto

With offices in
Argentina   Austria   Brazil   Chile   Czech Republic   France   Greece
Guatemala   Hungary   Italy   Japan   Poland   Portugal   Singapore
South Korea   Switzerland   Thailand   Turkey   Ukraine   Vietnam

Published by Oxford University Press, Inc.
198 Madison Avenue, New York, New York 10016

www.oup.com

Library of Congress Cataloging-in-Publication Data
Otis, John D.
Managing chronic pain : a cognitive-behavioral therapy approach :
therapist guide / John D. Otis.
p. cm. — (TreatmentsThatWork)
Includes bibliographical references.
ISBN 978-0-19-532916-2
1. Chronic pain.
2. Cognitive therapy.
I. Title. II. Series: Treatments that work.
[DNLM: 1. Chronic Disease—therapy. 2. Pain—therapy. 3. Cognitive
Therapy—methods.
WL 704 O88m 2007]
RB127.O788 2007
616′.0472—dc22   2007014190

9 8 7 6 5 4

Printed in the United States of America
on acid-free paper

About Treatments *ThatWork*™

Stunning developments in healthcare have taken place over the last several years, but many of our widely accepted interventions and strategies in mental health and behavioral medicine have been brought into question by research evidence as not only lacking benefit but perhaps inducing harm. Other strategies have been proven effective using the best current standards of evidence, resulting in broad-based recommendations to make these practices more available to the public. Several recent developments are behind this revolution. First, we have arrived at a much deeper understanding of pathology, both psychological and physical, which has led to the development of new, more precisely targeted interventions. Second, our research methodologies have improved substantially, such that we have reduced threats to internal and external validity, making the outcomes more directly applicable to clinical situations. Third, governments around the world and healthcare systems and policymakers have decided that the quality of care should improve, that it should be evidence-based, and that it is in the public's interest to ensure that this happens (Barlow, 2004; Institute of Medicine, 2001).

Of course, the major stumbling block for clinicians everywhere is the accessibility of newly developed evidence-based psychological interventions. Workshops and books can go only so far in acquainting responsible and conscientious practitioners with the latest behavioral healthcare practices and their applicability to individual patients. This new series, Treatments *ThatWork*™, is devoted to communicating these exciting new interventions to clinicians on the frontlines of practice.

The manuals and workbooks in this series contain step-by-step detailed procedures for assessing and treating specific problems and diagnoses. But this series also goes beyond the books and manuals by providing ancillary materials that will approximate the supervisory process in assisting practitioners in the implementation of these procedures in their practice.

In our emerging healthcare system, the growing consensus is that evidence-based practice offers the most responsible course of action for the mental health professional. All behavioral healthcare clinicians deeply desire to provide the best possible care for their patients. In this series, our aim is to close the dissemination and information gap and make that possible.

This therapist guide, and the companion workbook for patients, addresses the management of chronic pain. Chronic pain can accompany a number of diseases and neuropathic conditions, as well as be the result of injury. It can not only limit a person's physical functioning, but can also severely affect psychosocial functioning. It often takes a significant toll on individuals and has implications for high costs for the healthcare system.

This guide is based on a cognitive-behavioral therapy (CBT) approach to chronic pain management. CBT has been shown to be effective for chronic pain management across a variety of pain conditions. Each session of this program presents a new skill to help the patient cope with chronic pain. Techniques include progressive muscle relaxation, cognitive restructuring, and stress management, among others.

The management of chronic pain with CBT can improve a patient's quality of life and decrease reliance on medical interventions. Offering a breadth of techniques in a user-friendly format, this guide is a valuable resource for therapists.

David H. Barlow, Editor-in-Chief,
Treatments *That Work*™
Boston, Massachusetts

References

Barlow, D.H. (2004). Psychological treatments. *American Psychologist, 59,* 869–878.

Institute of Medicine. (2001). *Crossing the quality chasm: A new health system for the 21st century.* Washington, DC: National Academy Press.

Contents

Chapter 1 | *Introductory Information for Therapists*

Background Information and Purpose of This Program

This manual is designed to be used by psychotherapists engaged in the treatment of individuals with chronic pain. It is written from a cognitive-behavioral perspective, as this approach has been found to be highly effective when working with patients who have chronic pain. An emphasis is placed on behavioral activation and changing negative thoughts associated with pain. This manual is evidence-based and incorporates those aspects of pain management that have yielded the most positive clinical outcomes. The strategies presented here have been utilized for years in clinical practice. Several of the techniques included are not unique to the practice of pain management and are often used when treating other conditions. However, this manual provides guidance for tailoring the presentation of these techniques (e.g., relaxation training, cognitive restructuring, stress management) to the specific needs of patients with chronic pain. Throughout the text, examples are included that are relevant and that have been found to resonate with patients who have pain. Sample dialogues are provided to assist the therapist in presenting key information to the patient. The therapist guide and corresponding workbook are organized by session and include educational materials and homework forms.

Information on Chronic Pain

Although pain is typically a transient experience, for some people pain persists past the point where it is considered an adaptive reaction to an acute injury and results in emotional distress and increased use of healthcare system resources. Consistent with a biopsychosocial model of illness, individuals with chronic pain often report that pain interferes with their ability to engage in occupational, social, or recreational activities. Their inability to engage in these reinforcing activities may contribute to increased isolation, negative mood (e.g., feelings of worthlessness and depression), and physical deconditioning, all of which in turn can contribute to the experience of pain. Over time, these types of negative cognitive and behavioral patterns can become highly resistant to change.

Pain is currently defined as an unpleasant sensory and emotional experience associated with actual or potential tissue damage, or described in terms of such damage (IASP, 1994). One way in which the experience of pain can be described is in terms of its duration. Pain that is short-lived and resolves on its own over time, such as pain associated with a minor burn, a cut, or a broken bone, is referred to as "acute pain." Pain that persists for an extended period of time (i.e., months or years), that accompanies a disease process, or that is associated with a bodily injury that has not resolved over time may be referred to as "chronic" pain (Classification of Chronic Pain, 1994).

Pain is one of the most common complaints made to primary care providers (Gureje, Von Korff, Simon, & Gater, 1998; Otis, Reid, & Kerns, 2005) and has significant implications for healthcare costs. In fact, the National Institute of Health identified chronic pain as the costliest medical problem in America, affecting nearly 100 million individuals (Byrne & Hochwarter, 2006). According to the Centers for Disease Control and Prevention's annual report, one in four adults say they suffered from a day-long episode of pain in the past month, and one in 10 adults reported pain lasting one year or more (CDC, 2006). Over 20% of all medical visits and 10% of all drug sales are pain-related (Max, 2003). In occupational contexts, chronic pain is not only a significant source of absenteeism, but also a major factor in reducing productivity while at work. Indeed, approximately half of all employees experience pain while on the job, with individuals whose work involves repetitive movement or heavy lifting being affected in greater numbers (Byrne & Hochwarter, 2006). It has been estimated that pain results in $79 billion annually in lost worker productivity (Max, 2003). A recent study estimated that the total healthcare expenditures for back pain alone reached over $90.7 billion in 1998 (Xuemei, Pietrobon, Sun, Liu, & Hey, 2004). Overall, the total direct and indirect costs of chronic pain in the United States have been estimated to be between $150 billion and $260 billion annually (Byrne & Hochwarter, 2006). These statistics led the 108th U.S. Congress to formally declare the 10-year period beginning January 1, 2001, the "Decade of Pain Control and Research" (CDC, 2006).

Types of Pain

Pain can be divided into two broad categories, nociceptive pain and neuropathic pain.

Nociceptive Pain

There are two types of nociceptive pain: somatic and visceral. Somatic pain is caused by the activation of pain receptors on the surface of the body such as the skin (cutaneous tissues) or tissues that are deeper such as muscle (musculoskeletal tissues). When pain occurs in the musculoskeletal tissues, it is called deep somatic pain. Deep somatic pain is usually described as "dull" or "aching" but localized. This type of pain is often expressed by people who "overdo it" and strain muscles when performing physical activity or exercising. Surface somatic pain is usually sharper and may have a burning or pricking quality. Common causes of surface somatic pain include postsurgical pain or pain related to a cut or burn. "Viscera" refers to the internal areas of the body that are enclosed within a cavity. Visceral pain is caused by activation of pain receptors resulting from infiltration, compression, extension, or stretching of the chest, abdominal, or pelvic viscera. Visceral pain is not well localized and is usually described as "pressure-like, deep squeezing." Examples of visceral pain include pain related to cancer, bone fracture, or bone cancer.

Neuropathic Pain

Neuropathic pain is a neurological disorder resulting from damage to nerves that carry information about pain. Neuropathic pain is reported to feel different from somatic or visceral pain and is often described using words such as "shooting," "electric," "stabbing," or "burning." It may be felt traveling along a nerve path from the spine into the arms and hands or into the buttocks or legs. Neuropathic pain has very different medication treatment options from other types of pain. For example, opioids (e.g., morphine) and nonsteroidal anti-inflammatory medications (NSAIDs) (e.g., ibuprofen) are usually not effective in relieving neuropathic pain. Medication treatments for neuropathic pain also include nerve block injections and a variety of interventions generally used for chronic pain. Examples of neuropathic pain conditions include phantom limb pain, postherpetic neuralgias, and other painful neuropathies (e.g., diabetes or alcohol-related). For the purpose of this treatment, it is important to note that patients with either neuropathic pain or nociceptive pain conditions can respond to cognitive-behavioral therapy (CBT).

Chronic Pain

Pain can occur in many parts of the body, each with its own prevalence, patterns, and presenting characteristics. However, some pain conditions are more common than others. Chronic low back pain is the most common chronic pain condition, affecting 15% to 45% of adults annually and at least 70% of adults over a lifetime (Anderson, 1997). Back pain is the most common cause of job-related disability and a leading contributor to missed work. Most low back pain follows injury or trauma to the back, but pain may also be caused by degenerative conditions such as arthritis or disc disease (protruding, herniated, or ruptured disc), sciatica, or osteoporosis or other bone diseases.

Headaches represent another large category of painful conditions. Tension headaches are the most common and affect 38% to 78% of people (Rasmussen, Jensen, Schroll, & Olsen, 1991). The pain is typically located in the forehead, neck, and shoulder areas, and many people describe the feeling as having a tight band around their head. Factors that can contribute to tension headaches include stress, skipping meals, or lack of exercise. Thus, treatment often includes cognitive-behavioral stress management training and relaxation.

Migraine headaches affect 18% of women and 6% of men (Lipon, Stewart, Diamond, Diamond, & Reed, 2001). They are often preceded or accompanied by a sensory warning sign called an "aura," such as flashes of light, blind spots, or tingling in the extremities. They are often accompanied by other signs and symptoms such as nausea, vomiting, and extreme sensitivity to light and sound. They may be localized behind one eye, and they are associated with intense pain.

Fibromyalgia syndrome (FMS) consists of a set of unexplained physical symptoms with general pain and hypersensitivity to palpation at specific body locations called "tender points." In addition, patients with FMS often report a range of functional limitations and psychological dysfunction, including persistent fatigue, sleep disturbance, stiffness, headaches, irritable bowel disorders, depression, anxiety, cognitive impairment, and general malaise sometimes referred to as "fibro fog" (Baumstark & Buckelew, 1992). FMS occurs predominately in adults and has a female-to-male ratio of 7 to 1 in those seeking treatment. While the cause of FMS is unknown, there are many triggering events thought to precipitate its onset, including viral or bacterial infection, physical or psychological trauma, or the development of another disorder such as rheumatoid arthritis, lupus, or hypothyroidism.

Development of This Treatment Program and Evidence Base

The primary goal of CBT for pain is to promote the adoption of an active problem-solving approach to tackling the many challenges associated with the experience of chronic pain. A shift from a perspective of helplessness with regard to these challenges to one of personal responsibility, self-control, and confidence is encouraged. The cognitive-behavioral approach is informed by the understanding that people generally do not stop being active because of pain, but because they have become adjusted to the idea that they are physically "disabled." Thus, CBT for chronic pain involves challenging those beliefs and teaching patients ways of safely reintroducing enjoyable activities into their lives. This can be a particularly daunting task when thoughts related to disability have been in place for many years. There are several key components to CBT for chronic pain, including cognitive restructuring (i.e., teaching patients how to recognize cognitive errors and change maladaptive thoughts related to pain into more adaptive, positive thoughts), relaxation training (e.g., teaching diaphragmatic breathing, visual imagery, progressive muscle relaxation), time-based activity pacing (i.e., teaching patients how to become more active without overdoing it), and graded homework assignments designed to decrease patients' avoidance of activity and reintroduce a healthy, more active lifestyle. Since individuals who experience chronic pain often report reduced activity levels and declines in social role functioning, CBT also focuses on promoting patients' increased activity and productive functioning using techniques such as exercise homework, activity scheduling, and graded task assignments (i.e., gradually increasing activity toward an identified goal).

Empirical Support

Cognitive and behavioral interventions have enjoyed considerable empirical support for their efficacy in ameliorating chronic pain associated with a variety of medical conditions (Compas, Haaga, Keefe, Leitenberg, & Williams, 1998). In a frequently cited meta-analysis of 25 randomized controlled trials of CBT for pain management, Morley, Eccleston, and Williams (1999) concluded that CBT is effective, as it resulted in significantly greater changes for the domains of the pain experience, cognitive coping and appraisal (positive coping measures), and reduced behavioral expression of pain when compared with alternative active treatments. In a recent randomized controlled trial of CBT conducted by Turner, Mancl, and Aaron (2006), patients completing a four-session cognitive-behavioral intervention for temporomandibular pain showed significant reductions in pain, interference, jaw function, and depression when compared with patients assigned to an education/attention control curriculum. Further, in a meta-analysis of 22 randomized controlled trials of psychological treatments for noncancerous chronic low back pain, cognitive-behavioral and self-regulatory treatments specifically were found to be efficacious (Hoffman, Papas, Chatkoff, & Kerns, 2007). Finally, while there are few studies examining the effectiveness of psychological treatments for pain in children and adolescents, a meta-analysis of 18 randomized controlled trials indicated that psychological treatments, principally relaxation and CBT, are effective in reducing the severity and frequency of chronic headache in children and adolescents (Eccleston, Morley, Williams, Yorke, & Mastroyannopoulou, 2002).

Risks and Benefits of This Treatment Program

The potential benefits of this program include improved physical functioning and reduced disability, improvements in mood and reduced anxiety associated with activity, a reduction in pain, and improved relations with family/spouse/significant other. CBT for chronic pain management is a very interactive treatment that often involves patients becoming more physically active. As a result, some patients may experience increased muscle soreness. In addition, patients may notice that as their functioning improves it may have an impact on long-standing identified roles of family members. For example, the patient may prefer to do an activity for himself rather than having someone do it for him.

The Role of Medications

The goal of this program is to teach patients skills that they can use to help manage chronic pain on their own. However, patients who express a desire to participate should not be asked to stop taking their pain medications in order to become engaged in the program. Many patients initially start this program taking their regular regimen of pain medications, and once they acquire new skills, either they are able to discontinue medications or they notice that their medications work more effectively. In sum, it is often the case that when patients learn ways of managing pain on their own, they are able to reduce their reliance on pain medication.

If a patient begins this program and decides that he would like to change his medication, he should discuss any desired changes first with his physician.

As part of this program, therapists will be asking their patients to commit themselves to the time and effort needed to practice and learn the techniques covered. Clinical research has demonstrated that CBT can be of benefit to patients with chronic pain if they are engaged in the process of therapy. However, patients who are not engaged in treatment, or are not convinced that the investment of their time will pay off in the end, will be less likely to follow through with the treatment plan and are more likely to drop out of treatment after the first few sessions.

In order for therapists to be able to expect active participation in therapy from their patients, they will need to be able to present a clear and convincing rationale for this treatment. It is important that therapists take the time to read key articles and chapters related to pain management and review the treatment materials before each session. Reading and asking questions of supervisors or peers will enable therapists to gain confidence in their knowledge of pain management techniques, their ability to answer patients' questions, and the specific skills they have to offer to their patients.

It is also important that other individuals who are involved in the patient's care (e.g., members of an interdisciplinary pain management team, primary care providers) be kept up to date with the patient's progress in treatment. This can be accomplished by keeping regular patient progress notes that discuss treatment issues such as goals and goal accomplishment, coordinating goals with other providers (e.g., exercise compliance when the patient is participating in physical therapy, or medication compliance), and discussing patient progress in pain team meetings or through direct or electronic contact with providers. It is also sometimes beneficial to invite significant others and spouses of patients to sit in on the last few minutes of each session so that they are aware of the topics covered and can offer support and encouragement to the patient.

Outline of This Treatment Program

This treatment program is divided into 11 sessions, each of which is designed to help therapists teach patients a new skill for coping with chronic pain (e.g., relaxation, cognitive restructuring, activity pacing). The material in each chapter can be presented in the course of a 60-minute therapy session. Each chapter includes an outline of major topics to be covered in the session, educational information to be conveyed to the patient, and instructions on how to use the techniques. Sessions end with the assignment of homework and weekly goals.

Setting Therapy Goals

There are three types of goals that the therapist sets with the patient:

1. *Overall Treatment Goals:* These are the overall goals for the pain treatment program that are set in Session 1. It is important to set goals that are realistic and can be achieved over the next 11 therapy sessions, not goals that would require many months or years to achieve. In addition, the goals should be measurable (e.g., walking two miles a week, going to the gym) rather than vague (e.g., be a better person, learn to relax, or decrease pain). It is sometimes the case that the goals will need to be modified over the course of therapy either because the patient achieved the goal and would like to set another or the patient has given it more thought and has changed his mind about what he would like to work toward in therapy.

2. *Weekly Behavioral Goals:* These are small achievable goals set toward the end of each therapy session that help the patient to take steps toward achieving the overall treatment goals. For example, if the overall treatment goal is to walk 30 minutes on the treadmill daily, a weekly behavioral goal might be to walk 10 minutes on the treadmill four times a week. The behavioral goal can be increased in small steps until the overall treatment goal is reached.

3. *Homework Goals:* Weekly homework goals associated with the treatment session material are set toward the end of each session.

For example, in addition to having the weekly behavioral goal of walking 10 minutes on the treadmill four times a week, a patient may have the goal of performing diaphragmatic breathing daily for 10 minutes or using the cognitive restructuring form on three maladaptive thoughts.

Monitoring Homework Completion

At the beginning of each session time is spent evaluating the extent to which the patient was able to complete the goals set the previous week. After reviewing the homework the therapist works with the patient to complete the Weekly Goal Completion Form (see sample in Chapter 4 and blank copy in Chapter 3). The patient fills in the form and rates the extent to which he achieved his goal using a numerical rating scale from zero to 10. The consistent use of this form has been found to be a highly effective way of holding patients accountable for homework completion, recognizing success, and providing reinforcement. Therapists should be sure not to let patients underestimate their successes.

Adapting this Program for Groups

While this treatment program is currently formatted to be used on an individual basis, it may easily be adapted for use in a group format as well. Although group therapy can be challenging to implement with patients with chronic pain, there are several benefits to conducting treatment in a group. First, group treatment is more time-efficient for the therapist, who is able to provide treatment to anywhere from five to 10 participants at the same time. Second, group treatment provides a mechanism for participants to learn coping skills from other group members who may have similar pain complaints or who have had to overcome similar hurdles in coping with a painful medical condition. Third, it is often helpful for patients with chronic pain to see that they are not alone in dealing with the distress and disability that often accompany chronic pain. Furthermore, conducting treatment in a group format allows patients who have chronic pain to gain valuable social support from other group members.

There are several ways that this treatment program can be modified in order to be used in a group format. As with individual treatment, it is critical in the first session that the therapist presents a clear and convincing rationale for this treatment approach; otherwise, it is very likely that group attendance will decline significantly. The beginning of each session should include a review of each group member's homework from the previous week using the Weekly Goal Completion Form. Discussing success or difficulties with completing goals openly is an excellent way of eliciting support and comments from the other group members. Although the skills reviewed each session and the materials provided in the program do not require any modifications to be used in a group format, it is important to keep in mind that each group member will have his or her own overall treatment goals, which means that for each session there will need to be individually tailored behavioral goals. Sessions that involve the use of restructuring forms can be facilitated by the therapist using a dry-erase board or chalkboard so that all the group members can follow along as examples are reviewed. There may be some sessions that are of particular interest to some patients but not others. For example, some patients may be interested in learning about sleep, while others may have more issues with anger management. In these cases patients can be reminded to help support their fellow group members by providing suggestions for techniques that they have found effective.

Involvement of a Significant Other in Treatment

Patients with chronic pain are sometimes seen for psychological treatment only after they have had years of pain that has dramatically affected every aspect of their lives, including the lives of their families. Over time, family dynamics and roles can become maladaptive and highly resistant to change. Involving significant others in the process of therapy can be helpful in order to begin changing these maladaptive family patterns. For example, inviting a patient's spouse to participate in the pain assessment can be an effective way to gain perspective on the patient's typical coping strategies and how pain has affected the patient's life. It also communicates to the spouse that the therapist recognizes that pain has affected everyone in the family and that the therapist values their input. In addition to being included as part of the assessment, the spouse could also be invited to attend the last few minutes of each therapy session in order to learn about the skills that the patient will be practicing at home and the behavioral goals he will be working toward each week. By eliciting the spouse's support for reaching the goals and practicing the skills, the spouse may be able to provide additional encouragement and support for the patient.

Use of the Client Workbook

The client workbook will aid therapists in delivering this treatment. It contains psychoeducational information on chronic pain and stress and instructions to clients that follow the format of this guide. Each chapter corresponds to a particular session of treatment and provides outlines for mastering skills such as relaxation and cognitive restructuring. The workbook also includes copies of all monitoring forms and skill worksheets used during sessions and for completing home exercises. All forms intended for multiple use can be photocopied from the workbook or downloaded from the Treatments *ThatWork*™ Web site at www.oup .com/us/ttw.

Chapter 2 | *The Pain Evaluation*

Making First Contact

There are a number of ways in which patients may be referred to see a psychologist in order to learn pain management skills. Some patients will take the initiative to contact a therapist upon the recommendation of their orthopedic surgeon, anesthesiologist, neurologist, or other pain specialist. In other cases, the psychologist may be provided the name of a patient to contact in order to set up a pain assessment. In any case, while some patients will be anxiously awaiting your telephone call to set up an appointment, there will be others who think that no one believes their pain is real and that you are calling because someone thinks the pain is "all in their head." As a result, you may encounter resistance to setting up the initial appointment. What follows is a script that may be helpful in overcoming some of that resistance.

THERAPIST: Mr. Smith, your provider contacted us because she believes that you could use some additional skills to help you cope with your pain.

PATIENT: I'm not sure how you can be of any help to me. My pain is real, not in my head. I don't need a psychologist.

THERAPIST: Seeing us does not mean we think the pain is in your head. When you've had pain for a long time it can affect many areas of your life. It can have an impact on relationships with family and friends, it can affect your ability to work or engage in social activities, and it adds stress to everyday activities. You may have noticed some of these things yourself?

(The patient will typically agree and offer some examples of how pain has affected her life.)

THERAPIST: Sometimes, as a result of being in pain for a long time, people begin to feel down or feel anxious. These (depression and anxiety) are conditions that can actually make your pain feel worse.

(Again, the patient may express agreement with this statement.)

THERAPIST: We think it is important to treat the whole person, not just a pain site like a knee or a back. The goal of our first meeting is to gather a complete history of your pain and how it affects all areas of your life. We'll sit down and talk for a while, about 45 minutes to an hour, and then I'll ask you to fill out some questionnaires about your pain. After I have reviewed the information, we will speak again to develop the best plan for your treatment. How does that sound?

PATIENT: Well, does that mean that you are going to be taking away my pain medication?

THERAPIST: No. If you decide that you would like to try to learn some of the pain management skills that we can teach you, it does not mean that you will be taken off your pain medications. In fact, everything you learn can be used to help your medications work better.

PATIENT: Alright, then, I'll meet with you and see what you have to offer.

Patient Assessment

Whether a patient is receiving pain treatment as part of a research study or as part of a clinical practice, it is important that she receive a comprehensive pain assessment in order for the therapist to gain a thorough understanding of her pain condition and determine whether she could benefit from therapy. The assessment should include a history of the pain complaint(s) that has brought the patient to treatment, the impact of pain on her psychosocial functioning, her past and present efforts to cope with pain, and any environmental contingencies that may be affecting her pain experience. The assessment should be repeated after treatment has been completed in order to document any changes in pain, disability, or distress that have occurred. This will allow the therapist to assess the effectiveness of the treatment intervention and is a helpful way to demonstrate progress to the patient. The data may also be of benefit when a therapist wants to demonstrate the treatment effectiveness to insurance companies or referral sources seeking pain management expertise for their patients.

Pain Interview

The first part of the assessment involves performing a clinical interview in which the patient will have the opportunity to describe her pain condition and how pain has affected her life. This may take from 45 minutes to an hour to complete. A sample pain interview has been provided on the following pages. A blank copy of the Pain Interview can be found in the Appendix of this manual.

Begin the interview by obtaining a pain history (i.e., the patient's description of the presenting pain problem), including details regarding the pain location, onset of the pain complaint (e.g., sudden onset associated with an event versus gradual onset), words used to describe pain (e.g., stabbing, electric, dull), and temporal patterns or cycles associated with the pain (e.g., pain that is worse in the evening versus morning). As many patients will have multiple pain sites, some of this information may be different for each pain site. It is important to ask about past and present treatments/medications tried for pain relief (e.g., physical therapy, surgery, narcotics) and their effectiveness, as well as things that the patient has identified that make her pain increase or decrease. Note if the things identified by the patient are passive (e.g., medications and injections) versus active techniques (e.g., activity pacing).

Also ask the patient if she is currently engaged in any litigation related to pain, as this may affect the degree to which she engages in a treatment that could reduce her pain, thus weakening her court case. Patients should be asked about their goals for the future, since this will influence the goals set in therapy. The interview should include a brief psychosocial history (e.g., education, family or a spouse), as this will provide information on potential sources of support. Alcohol or recreational drug use can have a negative impact on treatment engagement and outcome and should be considered prior to engaging a patient in an active treatment for pain management such as CBT. Given the relationship between pain and mood, time should be spent obtaining a mental health

Figure 2.1 Example of Completed Pain Interview

Patient Name: _Amy Davis_

Age: _57_

Evaluation Date: _3/17/07_

Pain Location

Primary pain site: _Low back pain with intermittent pain radiating down into the left leg._

Secondary pain site: _Neck pain (intermittent/once a month)._

Details of Injury/Onset: _Fell off a step ladder while moving boxes at work. Worked for the rest of the afternoon but had difficulty getting out of bed the following morning. Went to the emergency room later that day._

Date of Onset

Back pain: _July 1988_

Neck pain: _Approximately December 2000_

Descriptors (e.g., burning, electric, sharp): _Back pain feels dull and throbbing, but the leg pain feels like an "electric shock." Neck pain feels sharp, intense, and jabbing._

Pain Rating (Scale: 0 = no pain; 10 = worst pain imaginable)

Current: _6_

Within the past 2 weeks: Average ___5___ ;   Worst ___9___ ;   Least ___2___

Intermittent _____ ;   Constant ___X___

Pain Medications and Effectiveness: _Gabapentin—prescribed by her anesthesiologist. Reported that it is not very effective for the back pain_

Previous Treatments (What things have you tried?)

Physical Therapy: _Yes, patient reported some benefit but it has been over seven years since her last appointment._

Chiropractic: _No._

Surgery: _Two back surgeries after the injury with limited benefit (1988, 1992)._

Psychology: _Spoke to a therapist a few times in the past about depressed mood._

Figure 2.1 *continued*

Other: _Acupuncture—the effects didn't last._

Temporal Cycles (Have you noticed any patterns to the pain?): _Back pain is worse in the morning but decreases after she performs stretching exercises. The pain never goes away and gradually increases toward the end of the day._

Pain Triggers (What makes your pain increase?): _Sitting or being on her feet for prolonged periods of time, lifting or bending to pick up something._

Pain Reducers (What makes your pain decrease?): _Hot showers, pain medication, distracting with something fun._

Coping Strategies (How do you cope with pain?): _Tries to push through the pain, but that sometimes backfires and causes more pain. Lying down in bed or on the couch but this can also cause pain._

Litigation pending? Yes _____; No __X__

Personal Goals (What are your goals for treatment?): _To be more active, less irritable toward family, and able to play with grandchildren. For pain to be tolerable. Better sleep._

Psychosocial History

Childhood (Where did you grow up? Who did you live with?): _Born in Boston, MA., and was the youngest of four children. No significant childhood traumatic events and no previous pain conditions as a child._

Education: _Completed high school and earned a BA in marketing from Wellesley College, Boston MA._

Past/Present Occupation: _Has worked in sales and marketing for a medium-sized business for the past 15 years. Currently employed but has been missing a significant amount of work due to pain. Considering applying for disability._

Marital/Family Relationship: _Married for 15 years, reported a supportive spouse. Three grown children, married with children._

Figure 2.1 *continued*

Living Situation (Where do you live? With whom? How do they respond to you when you're in pain?):

Currently lives with her spouse, who is approaching retirement. She described their relationship as positive and that he is typically sympathetic when it comes to her pain, but he occasionally expresses frustration that she has become so limited.

Recreational Activities: *She reported that she loved to garden but feels that she can no longer do it due to pain. No longer socializes or goes to lunch with her friends.*

Typical Day (Describe a typical day for you): *Has been missing significant amounts of work in the past few months due to pain. Spends most of the day watching TV or trying to read in order to avoid pain.*

Impact of Pain (How has pain impacted your life?): *She reported feeling that she is not the person that her husband married, and she expressed feeling guilty because of this. She reported feeling that pain had cheated her out of so many fun things.*

Substance Use

Past and Present Alcohol and/or Cigarette Use: *Quit smoking cigarettes 20 years ago. Reported minimal alcohol use (1 beer per month) and no heavier use in the past.*

Past and Present Recreational Drug Use: *Denied past or present use.*

Affective Status

Prominent Mood Disorders (Based on DSM-IV Criteria) (Have you noticed any changes in your mood? Have you been feeling depressed? Have you experienced any anxiety?):

Reported feeling moderately depressed for the past three months, difficulty falling asleep, feeling lethargic and reduced energy, irritability, decreased interest in previously enjoyable activities, and frequent crying.

Past or Present Participation in Individual or Group Therapy: *Individual therapy in 1987–1988 for depressed mood. Mostly talk therapy—some benefit—nothing since.*

Past/Present Psychiatric Hospitalizations: *None*

Psychopharmacological Medications: *Reported a trial of Prozac for six months in 1988 but did not like the side effects, so stopped taking it.*

history, including information on anxiety and depression. All of this information will be useful to other pain management specialists (e.g., anesthesiologists, neurologists, physical therapists) who may consult with you about the most appropriate ways to address the patient's pain.

Self-Report Measures

In order to supplement information obtained in the interview, the assessment can also include self-report measures that have been validated with a chronic pain population. Domains assessed typically include pain, disability, affective distress, and coping. One of the simplest and most effective ways of assessing a person's level of pain is to ask her to rate her pain on a zero-to-10 scale, with zero representing "no pain" and 10 representing "the worst pain imaginable." This type of rating is particularly useful when a psychologist needs to perform a brief assessment, such as when working in a physician's office or primary care setting (Jensen, Turner, Romano, & Fisher, 1999). The McGill Pain Questionnaire (MPQ; Melzack, 1975) is a self-report questionnaire consisting of 102 words separated into three major classes (the sensory, affective, and evaluative aspects of pain) and 16 subclasses. It is frequently used in studies of chronic, acute, and laboratory-induced pain, and its stability, reliability, and validity have been established (Reading, Everitt, & Sledmere, 1982).

If more time is available and a more comprehensive assessment of the patient's functioning is desired, the West Haven-Yale Multidimensional Pain Inventory (WHYMPI) is recommended (Kerns, Turk, & Rudy, 1985). The WHYMPI is a 52-item self-report questionnaire that is divided into three parts. Part I includes five scales designed to measure dimensions including perceived interference of pain, support or concern from spouse or significant other, pain severity, perceived life control, and affective distress. Part II assesses patients' perceptions of the degree to which spouses or significant others display Solicitous, Distracting, or Negative responses to their pain behaviors. Part III assesses patients' report of the frequency with which they engage in four categories of common everyday activities. Its brevity, validity/reliability, self-report nature, and ease of scoring make the WHYMPI ideal for both clinical and research purposes.

The coping strategies that individuals use in response to pain can be assessed using the Coping Strategies Questionnaire–Revised (CSQ-R; Riley, Robinson, & Geisser, 1999). Adequate internal validities for the six cognitive subscales (Diverting Attention, Reinterpreting Sensations, Catastrophizing, Ignoring Sensations, Praying and Hoping, Coping Self-Statements) and a behavioral scale (Behavioral Activities) have been demonstrated (Keefe, Crisson, Urban, & Williams, 1990). Another measure of coping that has been widely used in pain research is the Pain Catastrophizing Scale (PCS; Sullivan, Bishop & Vivek, 1995). The PCS asks patients to reflect on past painful experiences and to indicate the degree to which they experienced each of 13 thoughts or feelings when experiencing pain on a five-point scale from zero (not at all) to four (all the time). Measures of mood such as the Beck Depression Inventory (BDI; Beck, Steer, & Garbin, 1988), the State Trait Anxiety Inventory (STAI; Spielberger, Gorsuch, & Luschene, 1976), and the Pain Anxiety Symptom Scale (PASS; McCracken, Zayfert &, Gross, 1997) are frequently used in pain research and may be considered as part of a self-report assessment battery.

Self-report measures should be completed immediately after the interview while the patient is in a waiting area so that the patient does not gain assistance from significant others in completing them. Review the instructions for each self-report instrument with the patient and make sure that the patient understands them. Explain to the patient that the information gained from the assessment will be reviewed with her at the follow-up appointment and will be used to tailor treatment to her individual needs. Patients often appreciate time spent reviewing the assessment results.

Chapter 3

Session 1: Education on Chronic Pain

(Corresponds to chapter 2 of the workbook)

Materials Needed

- Goal Setting Worksheet
- Weekly Goal Completion Form

Outline

- Review assessment results
- Discuss the impact of pain
- Explain the pain cycle
- Present the general goals for treatment
- Set overall behavioral goals for treatment
- Assign homework

Assessment Review

Use the first few minutes of the session to review the results of the self-report measures the patient completed as part of the pain assessment. Note the patient's areas of strength and adaptive ways of coping and the areas in which the patient could use additional skills. Mention to the patient that he will be asked to set goals at the end of the session and he may want to set some goals in the areas that need improvement.

Pain is defined as an unpleasant sensory and emotional experience associated with actual or potential tissue damage, or described in terms of such damage. Pain that persists for six months or longer in duration is typically referred to as "chronic" pain. This definition is significant for our discussion in that it acknowledges that there is an emotional component to pain. You can begin the conversation with a general statement such as:

> *For many people, chronic pain affects more than just their neck, shoulder, or back. It affects the way they work and the way they play. It can affect everything they do; it can even affect people's moods. Have you experienced any of this yourself?*

Patients are usually able to talk about the different ways that pain has affected their lives. These will generally fall under the broad categories of *activities* and *thoughts and feelings* (see examples provided).

Activities: Pain can affect a person's activity level and the types of work or social activities he performs, and this can have an impact on a person's experience of pain. For example, a person in pain may avoid socializing with others, call in sick to work, have a hard time getting out of bed, watch TV all day, etc. This can lead to decreased muscle tone, weight gain, and overall weakness. You may want to ask the patient the following questions:

- *Has pain affected your ability to engage in social activities or hobbies?*
- *Has pain affected your ability to work or function?*
- *When in pain, what kinds of activities do you usually do?*
- *Has limiting your activities resulted in any negative physical or social effects?*

Thoughts and Feelings: The way a person thinks (e.g., "Life is unfair," "I'm never going to get better") and feels (e.g., worthless, depressed, anxious) can have a big impact on his experience of pain. Research indicates that negative emotions or thoughts tend to increase the focus on pain so that it is more noticeable. Questions to ask the patient include:

Have you ever observed a relationship between your emotions and pain?

How do you feel emotionally on days in which you are experiencing a lot of pain?

Does anger, frustration, or sadness also increase with the pain?

What kinds of thoughts are associated with those feelings?

The Cycle of Pain, Distress, and Disability

The use of a pain cycle drawing is often an effective way of demonstrating the relationship between pain, distress (thoughts and feelings), and disability (behaviors). Refer to Figure 3.1 or draw the pain cycle as you sit with the patient. A copy of the figure can be found in Chapter 2 of the workbook as well.

This dialogue can be used when explaining the pain cycle:

When pain persists over time, you may develop negative beliefs about your pain (e.g., "This is never going to get better," "I can't cope with my pain") or negative thoughts about yourself (e.g., "I'm worthless to my family because I can't work," "I'm never going to recover"). As pain continues, you may avoid doing activities (e.g., work, social activities, or hobbies) for fear of further injury or increases in pain. As you withdraw and become less active, your muscles may become weaker, you may begin to gain or lose weight, and your overall physical conditioning may decline. This diagram shows how distress and disability feed back into pain and make it seem worse.

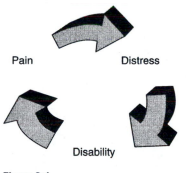

Pain   Distress

Disability

Figure 3.1
Pain Cycle

Ask the patient if he has noticed the pain cycle at work in his own life. Explain that this treatment will help him break the cycle of pain, distress, and disability.

General Goals of Treatment

Patients often feel that their pain is out of their control. This treatment teaches patients how to take back control by managing their thoughts, emotions, and behavior. This dialogue may help patients reconceptualize pain as something that is under their control:

Now that you know how important your thoughts and activities are in the experience of pain, it is important to realize that your thoughts and the things you do in response to pain are all under your control. By learning ways of addressing negative thoughts and emotions associated with pain, and ways of keeping active, you can take greater control over your pain rather than relying on physicians or medications for pain relief.

Ask the patient if he agrees with these statements. He may still have some doubts about his ability to take control. Explain that he will become more confident as the treatment progresses.

Next, present to the patient the general goals of treatment:

- Reduce the impact pain has on daily life
- Learn skills for coping better with pain
- Improve physical and emotional functioning
- Reduce pain and the reliance on pain medication

Explain to the patient that the program will help him achieve these goals by teaching him many techniques that people have found to be effective in helping them cope better with pain. Each of these techniques will be practiced in session and at home to see which ones work best for the patient. Emphasize that ongoing practice is essential to learning these new techniques and that homework is an important part of getting the most out of the program.

At this point you want to set some overall goals for therapy with your patient. This is important because these goals will help guide the weekly behavioral goals as discussed in Chapter 1. Get started by asking the patient to name some activities he would like to do more often, perhaps something he has not done in a while. Determine if the reintroduction of this activity is feasible given the condition of the patient. (You may need to consult with the patient's primary care provider, physician, or physical therapist in order to make this determination.)

Use the Goal Setting Worksheet to complete this task. See Figure 3.2 for a completed example of the worksheet. A blank copy is included on page 108. Identify areas for goal setting, reminding the patient of areas that need skill building according to assessment results. Discuss the importance of setting specific, rather than vague, goals for treatment. Ask the patient to try to identify at least three specific overall treatment goals. If needed, this task can be continued in the next session, but goals must be identified by the end of Session 2.

Goals should be:

1. Quantifiable behaviors (e.g., walk one mile, volunteer three times a week, garden every day versus goals such as decrease pain, be a better person, or improve mood)

2. In areas where the patient can reasonably expect change over the course of 11 sessions of treatment

For each of these goals, decide with the patient what would be some improvement, moderate improvement, and maximum improvement. Have patient record these on the Goal Setting Worksheet (Fig. 3.2) in Chapter 2 of the workbook. This will be helpful at the end of the program because it will allow you and the patient to determine the extent to which he has achieved the goals.

Explain to the patient that the overall treatment goals will be broken down into weekly behavioral goals. These small achievable goals will help the patient work step by step toward the overall goals. For example, if an overall treatment goal is to walk a mile every day, a weekly behavioral goal might be to buy a good pair of walking sneakers and walk a

Goal	Some Improvement	Moderate Improvement	Maximum Improvement
1. Walk 2 miles, 3 times a week	Walk around the block twice a week	Walk 1 mile 2 times a week	Walk 2 miles 3 times a week
2. Go fishing with my son every other week	Get all of my fishing gear together and pick out a fishing spot	Go fishing with my son once a month	Go fishing with my son every other week
3. Paint three times a week for an hour	Organize my paints and paint once a week for 30 minutes	Paint twice a week for 40 minutes	Paint three times a week for an hour
4. Clean out the garage	Get rid of all the trash in the garage	Organize all of the tools in the garage	Clean out the garage so that my car fits
5. Have lunch with a friend once a week	Have lunch with a friend once a month	Have lunch with a friend every other week	Have lunch with a friend once a week

Figure 3.2

Example of Completed Goal Setting Worksheet

quarter of a mile two mornings that week. The next week's goal might then be to walk a half-mile three mornings that week.

Work with the patient to choose one of his overall goals and help him break it down into a behavioral goal for the coming week. Have the patient record this goal in the space provided in the homework section of the workbook. Establishing this procedure for keeping track of homework assignments from the beginning of therapy will lessen the likelihood that the patient will forget his homework for the week. Also, record this goal yourself on the Weekly Goal Completion Form. This should be done at the end of each therapy session to ensure that you have a written record of the homework assigned that week. A blank form is included in this chapter. You may photocopy this form from the

Weekly Goal Completion Form

Session Number: _____

Please rate goal accomplishment for the week by marking the scale below: 0 (not at all accomplished) to 10 (completely accomplished). Please complete for each established goal.

Goal 1 _____

0 —— 1 —— 2 —— 3 —— 4 —— 5 —— 6 —— 7 —— 8 —— 9 —— 10

Notes: _____

_____

Goal 2 _____

0 —— 1 —— 2 —— 3 —— 4 —— 5 —— 6 —— 7 —— 8 —— 9 —— 10

Notes: _____

_____

Goal 3 _____

0 —— 1 —— 2 —— 3 —— 4 —— 5 —— 6 —— 7 —— 8 —— 9 —— 10

Notes: _____

_____

Goal 4 _____

0 —— 1 —— 2 —— 3 —— 4 —— 5 —— 6 —— 7 —— 8 —— 9 —— 10

Notes: _____

_____

Goal 5 _____

0 —— 1 —— 2 —— 3 —— 4 —— 5 —— 6 —— 7 —— 8 —— 9 —— 10

Notes: _____

_____

book or download multiple copies from the Treatments *That Work*™ Web site at www.oup.com/us/ttw. You will use this form to review the patient's progress at the beginning of each session. An example of a completed form can be found in Chapter 4.

Homework

✎ Have patient complete the Things That Affect My Pain worksheet in the workbook.

✎ Have patient work toward completing the weekly behavioral goal set at the end of the session.

Chapter 4

Session 2: Theories of Pain
and Diaphragmatic Breathing

(Corresponds to chapter 3 of the workbook)

Materials Needed

- Weekly Goal Completion Form

Outline

- Review homework
- Present theories of pain
- Introduce relaxation techniques
- Teach diaphragmatic breathing
- Assign homework

Homework Review

Look over the patient's completed Things That Affect My Pain work-sheet and comment on things with an external locus of control (e.g., more medications, bad weather) versus things that are more internal (e.g., pacing myself, doing something to distract myself, keeping active, not overdoing it). Reinforce any positive coping strategies listed and note that we want to develop more things that the patient can do personally to control her pain. Complete the Weekly Goal Completion Form with the patient for each homework assignment, including weekly behavioral goals. See Figure 4.1 for an example of a completed form. A blank form is included in Chapter 3. Since you will use this form on a weekly basis,

Session Number: _____1_____

Please rate goal accomplishment for the week by marking the scale below: 0 (not at all accomplished) to 10 (completely accomplished). Please complete for each established goal.

Goal 1 _Walk around the block twice a week._____

0 —— 1 —— 2 —— 3 —— 4 —— ⑤ —— 6 —— 7 —— 8 —— 9 —— 10

Notes: _Only walked around the block once a week._____

_____

Goal 2 _Complete Things That Affect My Pain worksheet._____

0 —— 1 —— 2 —— 3 —— 4 —— 5 —— 6 —— 7 —— 8 —— ⑨ —— 10

Notes: _Had trouble coming up with things that decrease pain._____

_____

Goal 3 _____

0 —— 1 —— 2 —— 3 —— 4 —— 5 —— 6 —— 7 —— 8 —— 9 —— 10

Notes: _____

_____

Goal 4 _____

0 —— 1 —— 2 —— 3 —— 4 —— 5 —— 6 —— 7 —— 8 —— 9 —— 10

Notes: _____

_____

Goal 5 _____

0 —— 1 —— 2 —— 3 —— 4 —— 5 —— 6 —— 7 —— 8 —— 9 —— 10

Notes: _____

_____

Figure 4.1
Example of Completed Weekly Goal Completion Form

you may photocopy it from the book or download multiple copies from the Treatments *ThatWork*™ Web site at www.oup.com/us/ttw.

Theories of Pain

This session begins with an educational component designed to inform the patient about our current understanding of pain. Education increases patient understanding and confidence in talking about pain and encourages patients to take a more active role in treatment.

Specificity Theory

The specificity theory suggests that the amount of pain a person feels is directly related to the amount of tissue damage that has occurred. According to this theory, pain should stop when the tissue has healed. However, there are several problems with this theory:

1. Many people continue to feel pain after injuries have healed. For example, patients who undergo the amputation of a limb may experience phantom pain or discomfort seemingly caused by the missing limb. If there is a direct relationship between pain and tissue damage, this should not happen.

2. People with similar amounts of tissue damage experience different levels of pain. This suggests that there is something unique about every person that affects the amount of pain experienced.

3. Some people with very little tissue damage feel a great deal of pain, while others with considerable tissue damage feel no pain. The following story can help to illustrate this point.

Dr. Beecher, a physician at Massachusetts General Hospital in Boston, was stationed in Normandy, France, during World War II. While seeing his patients he noticed a difference in the pain complaints of injured civilians and soldiers. Dr. Beecher observed that soldiers sometimes complained of little pain when injured in combat despite having significant wounds (e.g., bullet wounds). Civilians, on the other hand, would report greater pain after sustaining less significant traumas (e.g., a splinter under the finger-

nail). Dr. Beecher reasoned that the thoughts that the person was having at the time were an important factor in the experience of pain.

Ask the patient if she can imagine the kinds of things the soldiers may have been thinking after they were wounded. How about the civilians? Reinforce the patient for examples given. Continue, citing the following examples if the patient has not given these:

For example, a soldier might have had thoughts to distract his attention from the pain—perhaps concerns for the lives of his comrades, or hopes of going stateside for a few weeks as a result of his injury. The soldier also knew that getting injured was to be expected in war. For the civilian, the injury could represent the most significant trauma ever experienced, and there might be more uncertainty as far as treatment outcome, lost wages, and the future. Thus, the civilian might focus more attention on the pain sensations.

The Gate Control Theory

The gate control theory (Melzack & Wall, 1965) was developed in the early 1960s by Ronald Melzack and Patrick Wall to account for the importance of the mind and brain in pain perception. The theory had a significant impact on the study of pain because it recognized that psychological factors can have important roles in the experience of pain. Use the following information to present the theory to the patient (see Figure 4.2). When you are injured, a signal travels from the site of injury through nerve fibers to the spinal cord and then up to the brain. The brain interprets the signal about tissue damage, and you perceive pain. The amount or severity of tissue damage is just one thing that influences the amount of pain we perceive. Researchers know that other factors influence the amount of pain we feel as well, especially in the case of chronic pain. In fact, most patients with chronic pain have noticed that their pain seems to increase or decrease on occasions when there is little evidence for change in the amount of tissue damage.

According to the gate control theory, the experience of pain is not simply the result of the interpretation of nerve impulses sent directly from sensory neurons to the brain. Rather, messages related to pain or

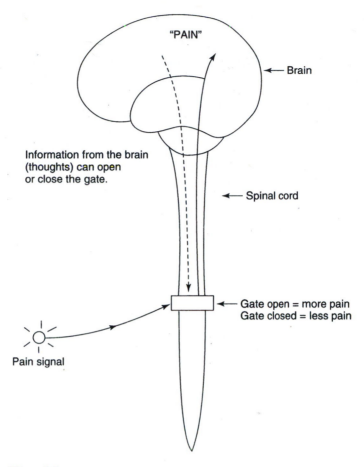

"PAIN"

Brain

Information from the brain
(thoughts) can open
or close the gate.

Spinal cord

Gate open = more pain
Gate closed = less pain

Pain signal

Figure 4.2
The Gate Control Theory

injuries can be modified by other incoming stimuli before reaching the brain. The theory suggests that a type of "gate mechanism" in the dorsal horn of the spinal cord modulates the pain signal. The gate opens and closes depending on feedback from other nerve fibers in the body. This includes descending neural impulses from the brain related to an individual's thoughts or mood (e.g., anxiety or depression). The opening and closing of the gate modifies how much information is sent to the brain from an injured area. Negative thoughts open the gate, which lets more pain information through, while positive thoughts close the gate and restrict the pain message. The result is that pain signals can be intensified, reduced, or even blocked on their way to the brain.

Table 4.1 Things that Open the Gate

Physical	Degenerative changes, muscle tension, drug abuse
Cognitive	Attention to pain, thoughts about uncontrollability of pain, beliefs about pain as a mysterious, terrible thing
Emotions	Depression, fear/anxiety, anger
Activity	Too much or too little activity, poor diet and other health behaviors, imbalance between work, social, and recreational activity
Social	Little support from family and friends, others focusing on your pain, others trying to protect you too much

After explaining the basics of the theory, use the following sample dialogues to increase the patient's understanding.

1. *Have you ever noticed that pain seems to increase at times when you are bored or unoccupied (e.g., at night while you are in bed), or when you are experiencing negative thoughts and emotions like anxiety, anger, and depression? Negative thoughts/emotions and attention to pain tend to hold the pain gate open.*

2. *Have you noticed that at other times, such as when you are distracted or doing enjoyable activities (e.g., watching a movie, socializing with friends, or doing something fun), you may not experience as much*

See tables 4.1 and 4.2 for a more complete list of things that open and close the pain gate.

Table 4.2 Things that Close the Gate

Physical	Drugs, surgery, reduced muscular tension
Cognitive	Distraction or external focus of attention, thoughts of control over pain, beliefs about pain as predictable and manageable
Emotions	Emotional stability, relaxation, and calm, positive mood
Activity	Appropriate pacing of activity, positive health habits, balance between work, recreation, rest, and social activity
Social	Support from others, reasonable involvement from family and friends, encouragement from others to maintain moderate activity

pain? That's because information from the brain is competing with information from the injury and closing the gate.

3. *Have you ever bumped your head or shin and then rubbed it? Did you notice that after you rubbed it the pain went away? When you rub the injured area you are actually stimulating sensory nerves that compete with the information carried by the pain nerves. The sensory information from those nerves closes the gate so less pain information can get through to the brain. This is also the reason that products like Bengay® require that you rub them in for them to work best. Stimulation of these nerves is the basis for the effectiveness of the TENS (Transcutaneous Electrical Nerve Stimulation) unit, acupuncture, and spinal cord stimulators.*

Relaxation Techniques

Relaxation is a skill individuals can use to gain some control over many functions of the body. In fact, some people can learn to change their blood pressure, heart rate, and other bodily functions normally thought to be beyond our control. The practice dates back thousands of years to Eastern religions that described the many health and spiritual benefits of learning to relax the mind and body. Over the past century many of these techniques have been adopted by Western culture. Research has demonstrated that relaxation can have many benefits, such as increased energy, decreased muscle tension and fatigue, improved sleep, lower blood pressure, and decreased pain. Patients often think that learning to relax means that they have to slow down or be less productive, but in fact if they are relaxed they can think more clearly and function better.

Briefly describe the three techniques that will be taught as part of this program:

- Diaphragmatic breathing

- Progressive muscle relaxation (see Chapter 5)

- Visual imagery (see Chapter 5)

Introduce the patient to diaphragmatic breathing and practice the technique in the session before assigning it as homework.

Therapist Note

■ *Be aware that relaxation may feel extremely uncomfortable for some people. For example, individuals who have experienced a traumatic event may not be accustomed to letting their guard down enough to relax. For these individuals, relaxation may have the effect of allowing negative thoughts and emotions to come rushing to the surface.* ■

Explain that learning to breathe correctly is probably the easiest and most effective method of learning how to relax and help reduce pain. Although breathing is automatic, as people get older they sometimes develop the habit of taking short shallow breaths. This often results from increased muscle tension in times of stress or pain. This type of breathing delivers less oxygen to the body and can cause the chest and shoulder muscles to work even harder.

A different way of breathing is "diaphragmatic breathing," which uses the muscles in the diaphragm and abdomen. The diaphragm is a dome-shaped muscle located right under the rib cage between the chest cavity and the stomach cavity. During correct diaphragmatic breathing the diaphragm is tightened and pulls the lower part of the lungs down so that more air can be inhaled. On the inhale, the abdomen swells, the rib cage expands, and at the end of the inhalation the upper chest expands. Tell the patient that if she ever watches babies or small children sleep, she will notice that it is their bellies, not their chests, that rise and fall as they breathe.

Steps to Diaphragmatic Breathing

1. Set up a "relaxation area":

   First, find a quiet place where you will not be disturbed. If needed, take the phone off the hook and tell others to give you this time alone. Loosen any tight clothing, or change into comfortable clothes. Next, sit with your feet flat on the floor and your hands in your lap or on the arms of the chair. You don't want to lie down because you might fall asleep, and learning can only occur if you are awake. Make sure you start out in a comfortable position.

2. Monitor:

   Place one hand on your abdomen and one hand on your chest. Take a normal breath in and notice which hand moves the most. Most likely it will be the hand on your chest, and this indicates that you tend to breathe shallow breaths from your chest as mentioned. Now try to take a breath from your abdomen. You might feel as though you are pushing your stomach out, and that is the way it should feel.

   An alternative way to monitor breathing is to ask the patient to place both of her hands across her abdomen so that the tips of the middle fingers are just touching near the center of the stomach. If the patient breathes in correctly, the tips of the fingers should separate.

3. Practice:

   Now close your eyes if you are comfortable doing so. Take a deep breath in through your nose slowly for a count of three and then exhale for a count of three from your mouth. Your exhalation should be as long in duration as your inhalation.

Practice taking breaths with the patient and ask her to continue for a minute at a comfortable pace. Remind the patient to breathe in through the nose for a count of three and out through the mouth for a count of three.

Address any concerns and modify the instructions as needed. For example, some patients may report feeling dizzy when concentrating on their breathing. If this occurs, ask the patient to breathe less deeply and at a more normal rate. Try using some of the following statements (autogenic phrases) to help the patient relax while breathing:

- *With each breath you feel your body sinking into the chair.*

- *With each breath, scan your body looking for any place where you might be holding tension, and let that area relax.*

■ *With each breath your body feels heavier and warmer.*

■ *With each breath you feel yourself becoming more relaxed and calm.*

■ *As you find yourself becoming more relaxed, you realize that you can feel this way whenever you want, just by taking the time to breathe deeply.*

It is recommended that patients try this technique at a consistent time and place that is best for learning (e.g., every morning before breakfast while sitting in the easy chair, sitting on the deck outside before the kids come home from school). Help them think of a time and place they can practice without being disturbed. Once they have practiced sufficiently and learned to use the breathing to become relaxed, they can start using the technique at other times during the day. In this way the ability to use the skill will become generalized to other times and places. In addition, after continued practice they will require less time to become relaxed.

A common objection raised by patients after being assigned breathing as homework is that they tried to use breathing when they were really "stressed out" but it didn't work. Let patients know from the beginning that until they have had a chance to really learn how to use breathing to relax, they should not expect that it will be very effective when up against very strong emotions. After all, they have had years to learn how to be stressed and only a few days of practice at relaxation. Ask patients to give themselves some time to practice.

Homework

Set the weekly behavioral goals with the patient and record on your Weekly Goal Completion Form for the next session. Have the patient write these in the space provided in the homework section of the corresponding workbook chapter.

✎ Have patient practice diaphragmatic breathing (e.g., five times a week for 15 minutes) using the Breathing Practice Log in the workbook.

✎ Have patient work toward completing the weekly behavioral goals set at the end of the session.

Chapter 5

Session 3: Progressive Muscle Relaxation and Visual Imagery

(Corresponds to chapter 4 of the workbook)

Materials Needed

- Weekly Goal Completion Form
- Imagery Form

Outline

- Review homework
- Conduct progressive muscle relaxation (PMR)
- Conduct visual imagery
- Assign homework

Homework Review

Discuss any difficulties the patient had in completing the diaphragmatic breathing assignment and the weekly behavioral goals. Reinforce attempts at practice and problem-solve around failure to complete homework. Complete the Weekly Goal Completion Form for each homework assignment.

The first half of this session introduces progressive muscle relaxation (PMR).

Therapist Note

📖 *Consult with the patient's physician or physical therapist about the extent to which the patient can safely be asked to tense his muscles. Do not ask the patient to tense muscles in areas that are in pain.* 📖

The most common response to an acute painful injury is to tighten the muscles. The tightening acts to limit movement, protect the body, and allow time for healing. However, when pain is chronic this response is not adaptive and does not promote healing. Increased muscle tension can also occur in response to anger, anxiety, frustration, and stress—all common emotions for people with chronic pain. It can also lead to feeling fatigued and impatient. Regardless of the source, increased muscle tension can amplify the experience of chronic pain. After presenting this information to the patient, the following dialogue can be used to introduce PMR:

> *Have you ever noticed when muscles in your neck, shoulders, or back are tense? These are common places that we carry tension; however, most of us are not aware of when these muscles are tense. The purpose of progressive muscle relaxation (PMR) is to help you to develop an awareness of when your muscles are becoming tense and learn to relax them before the tension becomes great.*

Give the patient general information on PMR. By going through groups of muscles in turn, tensing them for a few seconds, and very gradually releasing the tension, deeper-than-normal levels of muscle relaxation can be attained. As well as deepening physical relaxation and heightening our awareness of areas and levels of tension, this technique elicits the "relaxation response" and induces a general state of mental calm and physical relaxation. The basic procedure may take a few attempts to get used to, but once it is mastered the muscles can be relaxed rapidly.

How to Begin

As you did when preparing to do your breathing exercises, make your-self as comfortable as possible in a seated position. Sit up straight with good posture, hands resting in your lap. Begin diaphragmatic breath-ing. Now, we will begin tensing and relaxing specific muscle groups. For feet, legs, arms, and hands, we will tense one side at a time. If you are right-handed, start with your right side. If you are left-handed, start with your left side.

Statements to use to help patients become more engaged

- *Notice the difference in how that muscle feels.*

- *Notice how your muscles feel when they are relaxed compared to being tense.*

- *Feel the tension leaving your muscles and warmth moving over your body.*

Relaxation of the Feet

1. *Flex your foot by pulling your toes up toward your knees while your feet are on the floor.*

2. *Feel the tension building in your foot and hold it for three seconds.*

3. *Take a deep breath.*

4. *As you exhale, say the word "relax" and release the tension slowly, pay-ing close attention to the different sensations.*

Perform this twice and repeat with the other foot.

Relaxation of the Calves

1. *Contract the calf muscle by lifting the heel of your foot.*

2. *Feel the tension build and hold it for three seconds.*

3. *Take a deep breath.*

4. *As you exhale, say the word "relax" and release the tension gradually by letting your heel return to the floor. Notice the different sensations.*

Perform this twice and repeat with the other calf muscle.

Relaxation of the Knees and Upper Thighs

1. *Extend your leg out straight and tense your thigh muscle.*

2. *Feel the tension building in your thigh and hold it for three seconds.*

3. *Take a deep breath.*

4. *As you exhale, say the word "relax" and release the tension, lowering your leg to the floor.*

Perform this twice and repeat with the other thigh.

Relaxation of the Abdomen

1. *Observe your abdomen rising and falling with each breath.*

2. *Inhale deeply and tense the abdomen (stomach muscles).*

3. *Feel the tension and hold it for three seconds.*

4. *As you exhale, say the word "relax" and release the tension in your abdomen.*

Relaxation of the Hands

1. *Tightly clench your fist for about five seconds.*

2. *Focus on the sensations in your hand and examine the feelings of muscular tension.*

3. *Take a deep breath, and as you exhale release the tension slowly and gradually, allowing your fist to open and your fingers to move.*

4. *Take a few moments to allow feelings of relaxation to develop. Focus on the contrast between relaxation and tension.*

Perform this twice and repeat using the other hand.

Relaxation of the Forearms

1. *Turn your palm face up, make a tight fist, and curl it toward you.*

2. *Feel the tension build and hold it for three seconds.*

3. *Take a deep breath.*

4. *As you exhale, say the word "relax" and release the tension in your forearm and hand.*

Perform this twice and repeat with the other forearm.

Relaxation of the Biceps

1. *Bring your fist in toward your shoulder and tighten your bicep.*

2. *Feel the tension build and hold it for three seconds.*

3. *Take a deep breath.*

4. *As you exhale, say the word "relax" and release the tension in your bicep while also relaxing your forearm and unclenching your fist. Let your entire arm go completely relaxed.*

Perform this twice and repeat with the other bicep.

Relaxation of the Shoulders

1. *Draw the shoulder blades together (to midline of body).*

2. *Contract the muscles across the upper back.*

3. *Feel the tension build and hold it for three seconds.*

4. *Take a deep breath.*

5. *As you exhale, say the word "relax" and release the tension, letting the shoulder blades return to their normal position, almost as if a weight had been placed on them.*

Relaxation of the Jaw and Facial Muscles

1. *Clench your teeth together.*

2. *Tense the muscles in the back of your jaw.*

3. *Turn the corners of your mouth into a tight smile.*

4. *Wrinkle the bridge of your nose and squeeze your eyes shut.*

5. *Tense all facial muscles in toward the center of your face.*

6. *Take a deep breath.*

7. *As you exhale, say the word "relax" and release the tension in your jaw and face.*

Relaxation of the Forehead

1. *Raise your eyebrows up and tense the muscles across the forehead and scalp.*

2. *Feel the tension build and hold it for three seconds.*

3. *Take a deep breath.*

4. *As you exhale, say the word "relax" and release the tension.*

Whole Body Muscle Relaxation

1. *Focus on relaxation flowing from the top of your head:*

2. *Over your face*

3. *Down the back of your neck and shoulders*

4. *Over your chest and abdomen*

5. *Flowing through your arms and hands*

6. *Flowing through your hips and buttocks*

7. *Into your thighs, knees, and calves*

8. *Into your ankles and feet.*

9. *Continue to deep breathe quietly for a few minutes.*

Finishing the PMR Exercise

Take a few seconds to empty your mind and to allow the feelings of relaxation to spread throughout your body. Scan your body, and if you find any remaining tension, allow yourself to let go of it.

Count backward in your head from three to one:

3. *Become aware of your surroundings.*

2. *Move your feet, legs, hands, and arms. Rotate your head.*

1. *Open your eyes, slowly, feeling refreshed and relaxed.*

Ask the patient for feedback on the PMR exercise. Ask him to note areas where he found he was holding tension. If the patient reports pain in specific areas after this exercise, ask him to not tense that muscle group or to perform only mild tensing in that area. If the patient requests, you can make an audio recording of the PMR exercise for him to listen to at home. With continued practice the patient will become increasingly skilled at using PMR to become relaxed. Instead of performing PMR on individual muscles (e.g., hand, forearm, and biceps) the patient may be able to tense an entire muscle group, like an arm or leg, and achieve the same result.

Visual Imagery

In the second half of the session, guide the patient through a visual imagery exercise. The following dialogue can be used to introduce the technique:

Stress and tension can be reduced significantly by using your imagination and focusing on positive, healing images. The purpose of this technique is to help you create a relaxing image that you can think of on your own. The image can be any scene you like, but it must be a pleasant image that you can visualize. For example, some people like to imagine a beach scene, while others prefer to imagine being in the woods, vacationing with friends, or being in a warm kitchen with cookies baking in the oven. This technique requires practice and good concentration in order for the visual image to be effective.

Before beginning, take a few minutes to gather information on the image the patient wishes to imagine. Write down the patient's responses on the Imagery Form provided. You may photocopy this form from the book or download multiple copies from the Treatments *ThatWork*™ Web site at www.oup.com/us/ttw. As the therapist, you will be responsible for weaving this information together to guide the patient in imagining the place he has chosen.

Use the following instructions to conduct the visual imagery exercise with the patient.

Prepare

As you did when preparing to do your breathing exercises, make yourself as comfortable as possible in your chair. Now shift your focus to the image you have chosen. As we begin, take several deep breaths.

Allow time for the patient to become comfortable and take several deep breaths.

Describe the Image

As you begin to guide the patient through the image he has chosen, try to encourage his active involvement in the image using statements and suggestions such as:

■ *Notice what you hear right now.*

■ *As you take a deep breath, notice the smell of the air.*

■ *Reach out and touch things around you. (Notice how the sand/leaf feels as you hold it in your hand.)*

Imagery Form

Record information about the image in the spaces provided. Include specific details in order to help create the scene.

Place: *Where do you want to be? (e.g., beach, forest)*

_____

_____

Vision: *What do you see? (e.g., trees, grass, sun, people, animals)*

_____

_____

Smell: *What do you smell? (e.g., ocean, pine, flowers)*

_____

_____

Sounds: *What do you hear? (e.g., birds, sticks cracking, waves)*

_____

_____

Touch: *What do you feel? (e.g., cool breeze, warm sun, water)*

_____

_____

Taste: *What can you taste? (e.g., salty air, sweet berries, cool water)*

_____

_____

Other:

_____

_____

_____

- *Identify a path along which you travel as you journey through your place. (As you look back you notice your footprints in the sand where you have just walked along the shore; slowly a wave moves in and washes away the sand.)*

- *As you go through, you should be moving deeper and deeper into the image. You feel calm and peaceful here.*

- *Before you return, notice how your body feels; you will want to return to this feeling next time.*

Finish the Exercise

Take a few seconds to empty your mind and to allow the feelings of relaxation to spread throughout your body. Scan your body, and if you find any remaining tension, allow yourself to let go of it.

Count backward in your head from three to one:

3. *Become aware of your surroundings.*

2. *Move your feet, legs, hands, and arms. Rotate your head.*

1. *Open your eyes, slowly, feeling refreshed and relaxed.*

Homework

Set the weekly behavioral goals with the patient and record on your Weekly Goal Completion Form for the next session. Have the patient write these in the space provided in the homework section of the corresponding workbook chapter.

✎ Have patient practice PMR using the Progressive Muscle Relaxation Practice Log in the workbook.

✎ Have patient practice imagery using the Visual Imagery Practice Log in the workbook.

✎ Have patient work toward completing the weekly behavioral goals set at the end of the session.

Chapter 6 | *Session 4: Automatic Thoughts and Pain*

(Corresponds to chapter 5 of the workbook)

Materials Needed

- Weekly Goal Completion Form
- ABC Worksheet

Outline

- Review homework
- Explain automatic thoughts
- Discuss how thoughts lead to emotions
- Explore the relationship between emotions and pain
- Review list of cognitive errors
- Introduce the ABC Model
- Assign homework

Homework Review

Discuss any difficulties the patient had in practicing PMR or visual imagery at home. At this point the patient may express a preference for one relaxation technique (e.g., diaphragmatic breathing) over another. Encourage the patient to use whichever technique she prefers. Reinforce attempts at practice and problem-solve around failure to complete homework. Complete the Weekly Goal Completion Form for each homework assignment, including weekly behavioral goals.

Automatic Thoughts

This section lays down the foundation for the patient's understanding that positive and negative thoughts about an event determine the emotional response to the event, and that emotions can have an impact on physical health, including the experience of pain. The following dialogue can be used to introduce the concept of automatic thoughts:

Automatic thoughts are thoughts that we have immediately after getting any kind of information. They occur very quickly, and unless we make an effort to pay attention to them, we may not even be aware of them. We have automatic thoughts for EVERYTHING that goes on in our world, even for very trivial kinds of things. For example, let's say that after today's session you have arranged to meet a friend back at your place to have lunch. You go home and as you get closer to your door, you see that there's a piece of paper taped to the door. What kinds of automatic thoughts do you think you might have about that?

Prompt for things like the friend left a note to cancel, the friend left a note saying that she had to run an errand and would be right back, it's a note from UPS, etc. Explain that the kinds of automatic thoughts that we have are affected by the kinds of experiences we've had in our lives. So, for instance, if you have a lot of friends who let you down, you might be more apt to have an automatic thought that the note was from your friend canceling your lunch. Here is another example that may increase patient understanding:

Automatic thoughts can help us to make sense of the world. For instance, going back to the previous example, pretend that when you get home, instead of finding a note attached to your door, you see that the door is open, and you know that you locked it this morning. What kind of automatic thoughts would you have now?

Prompt for someone having broken in. Point out how that kind of automatic thought could be helpful because it would alert you to a potentially dangerous situation.

The next step is to explain to the patient how thoughts lead to emotions. For some people this will be the first time they have really thought about where emotions come from. Explain that though automatic thoughts have a purpose, they can sometimes be negative and based on faulty information. They can trigger even more negative thoughts that can have an impact on how we feel (emotionally and physically) and how we behave. Use the following dialogue to clarify:

> *You can probably remember a time when you became really upset about something, got really worked up about it emotionally, and then found out later that what you thought was happening wasn't even true. **The way you think about an event, either positively or negatively, determines the emotions you experience.** Negative thoughts lead to negative emotions, while pleasant emotions are caused by thinking pleasant thoughts.*

To make it more concrete and easy to follow, you could try drawing the chain of events out on a sheet of paper in front of the patient while talking about the relationship between thoughts and feelings (see Figure 6.1).

After delivering this information you may want to spend a few minutes reviewing examples from the patient's own personal experience where thoughts have led to specific positive and negative emotions. The following is an example that you can use to demonstrate the power of thoughts.

Situation A: *A car is speeding and cuts you off in traffic.*

- *What are you thinking about this person?*

- *What are you feeling?*

Figure 6.1
Chain of Events

Situation B: *Now suppose you know that the wife of the driver is in the backseat and she is about to have a baby. He is rushing to get her to the hospital down the street.*

■ *What are you thinking about this person?*

■ *How does that information change the way you feel?*

Note how the emotion may change from *anger* to *concern* once the thoughts about the person and his actions have changed.

Emotions and Pain

Now that the patient understands that thoughts lead to emotions, explore the relationship between emotions and pain. Research and clinical practice indicate that the link between negative emotions (e.g., anxiety and depression) and chronic pain is very strong. In fact, depression is a common and significant factor in the experience of chronic pain that is related to increased report of pain, lower pain tolerance, and increased disability. A high percentage of patients who seek treatment for their chronic pain are depressed.

Ask the patient if she has ever noticed a relationship between her emotions and her pain. Often a patient will tell you that she has noticed that when she feels upset or gets angry or frustrated her pain seems to get worse, but when she is happy or distracted she feels less pain or doesn't even notice pain. Reinforce the patient's observation of this relationship. If the patient is not able to see the relationship between thoughts, feelings, and pain, try using the following examples:

1. *People often report that when they are enjoying themselves with family or friends (playing a game of cards or having a laugh), they sometimes forget that they have a pain problem. Why do you think this might be the case?*

    Prompt for: "They are focusing on having a good time and not the pain."

2. *Consider that many professional athletes can play their sport while injured without experiencing significant pain. What do you think the athletes are thinking and feeling?*

Prompt for: "They are thinking about winning the game and not themselves."

Relate the patient's observation of the relationship between negative thoughts/emotions and pain (or these examples) to the gate control theory discussed in Session 2. Remind her that negative thoughts/emotions cause the gate to open so that more pain information gets to the brain, while positive thoughts/emotions cause the gate to close and result in less pain. Point out that since emotions can affect pain, and emotions are caused by how we think, we need to make sure that our thinking is accurate. We may often find that our negative thoughts are inaccurate, causing us to experience negative emotions and increased pain unnecessarily.

Cognitive Errors

Do a quick review of automatic thoughts. Remind the patient that we have automatic thoughts for everything that happens in our world and that these thoughts cause the emotions that we experience. Our emotions have an impact on us and can even make pain seem worse. The problem is that our automatic thoughts may be unreliable and based on faulty information. One way that we can manage pain is to learn to identify inaccurate and negative thoughts that contribute to negative emotions and increased pain.

Cognitive errors are ways of thinking that are based on faulty assumptions or misconceptions. Before learning how to correct cognitive errors with a process called "cognitive restructuring," it can be helpful to learn the types of errors in thinking that are the most commonly made. Introduce the list of cognitive errors with the following statement:

Let's first review the types of cognitive errors. As we go through the list, think of which errors may apply most to you. We all think in these ways from time to time, and you will probably notice that some of these ways of thinking look very familiar.

Review the complete list of cognitive errors with the patient and ask her to identify one of them that she or someone she knows has made in the past. Emphasize that making these types of errors is very common.

List of Cognitive Errors (Adapted from Burns, 1999)

1. *All-or-nothing thinking:* When you see things in all-or-nothing categories. For example, if your performance falls short of perfect, you see yourself as a total failure.

2. *Overgeneralization:* When you see a single negative event as a never-ending pattern. For example, if you do not do well at one thing, you think you are not good at anything.

3. *Mental filter:* When you pick out a single negative detail and dwell on it exclusively, so that your vision of all reality becomes darkened. A good metaphor is a drop of ink that discolors the entire glass of water.

4. *Disqualifying the positive:* When you reject positive experiences by insisting they "don't count" for some reason or another. In this way, you can maintain a negative belief that is contradicted by your everyday experiences.

5. *Jumping to conclusions:* When you make a negative interpretation of an event even though there are no definite facts that convincingly support your conclusion.
   a. *Mind reading:* When you arbitrarily conclude that people are reacting negatively to you, and you do not bother to consider other possible explanations for their behavior (e.g., they are tired, they had a rough day).
   b. *The fortune-teller error:* When you anticipate that things will turn out badly, and you feel convinced that your prediction is an already established fact. This prediction may in turn affect your behavior, making it a self-fulfilling prophecy.

6. *Binocular vision:* When you distort information in a way that no longer allows you to view the situation realistically.
   a. *Magnification:* When you exaggerate the importance of things (such as your goof-up, or someone else's achievement).
   b. *Minimization:* When you inappropriately shrink things (such as your own positive qualities or someone else's imperfections) until they appear tiny.

7. *Catastrophizing:* When you predict extreme and horrible consequences to the outcomes of events. For example, a turndown for

a date means a life of utter isolation. Or, making a mistake at work means you will be fired for incompetence and never get another job.

8. *Emotional reasoning:* When you assume that your negative emotions necessarily reflect the way things really are. You might think, "I feel it; therefore, it must be true."

9. *"Should" statements:* When you try to motivate yourself with "shoulds" and "shouldn'ts." "Musts" and "oughts" are also offenders. The emotional consequence to this type of statement is guilt. When you direct "should" statements toward others, you feel anger, frustration, and resentment.

10. *Labeling and mislabeling:* This is an extreme form of overgeneralization. Instead of describing your error, you attach a negative label to yourself: "I'm a failure," "I'm stupid." When someone else's behavior rubs you the wrong way, you attach a negative label to him: "He's an idiot." Mislabeling involves describing an event with language that is highly colored and emotionally loaded: "That was a total disaster," "This has ruined my life."

11. *Personalization:* When you see negative events as indicative of some negative characteristic of yourself, or you see yourself as the cause of some negative external event for which, in fact, you were not primarily responsible: "I should have caught the error in the report before it left my boss's desk," "I'm bad luck; my team loses every time I watch the game."

12. *Maladaptive thoughts:* When you focus on something that may in fact be true, but is nonetheless not helpful to focus on excessively: "My knee hasn't been the same since surgery," "I'm starting to lose my hair."

The ABC Model

Before patients can learn to restructure their negative thoughts, they first need to practice making the connection between the way they think about an event and the way it makes them feel. This can be accom-

Activating Event (Stressful Situation)	Beliefs (Automatic Thoughts)	Consequences (My Reactions)
I bend over to pick up a package and I get a big increase in my pain.	Why me? What did I do to deserve this? Now I'm in for a miserable day.	**Emotional:** Frustrated and angry
		Physical: Face feels hot and flushed
		Behavioral: Walk slowly so I don't cause more pain
I wake up in the middle of the night in pain.	I can't take this. This is terrible. My whole day is going to be ruined tomorrow.	**Emotional:** Sad and depressed
		Physical: Sweating, headache
		Behavioral: Watch TV for the rest of the night. Go in late to work in the morning.

Figure 6.2

Example of Completed ABC Worksheet

plished by using an ABC Worksheet (see Figure 6.2 for a completed example). A blank form is included in the workbook.

Have the patient follow along as you describe the three columns of the ABC Worksheet.

For column C, focus on the emotions, but also record the physical and behavioral consequences of thoughts.

A is for Activating Event: *This is the stressful situation that is happening.*

B is for Beliefs: *These are things you tell yourself. They are the thoughts you have about the situation.*

C is for Consequences: *These are the feelings and reactions you have in response to the Activating Event. These reactions can be emotional, physical, or behavioral, or all three.*

*For example: Let's say that pain wakes you up in the middle of the night. This is your **A** or Activating Event. You may be more aware of your emotions rather than your thoughts and beliefs at first, so if that is the case then just skip over to the **C** or Consequences column and record the emotions you are experiencing.*

*Now let's take a look at the **B** or the Beliefs and Automatic Thoughts you might have about this Activating Event. What are some of the thoughts you might have about awakening at night from a pain episode that are contributing to your emotions?*

*Okay, let's go back to column **C**. Can you think of other emotions that might be a consequence of your negative thoughts? What about physical and behavioral consequences? How does your body feel? How do you act?*

The take-home message for patients should be that if they are able to maintain more positive and healthy thoughts rather than negative thoughts, they can reduce the occurrence of negative emotions. This can also result in decreased pain.

Homework

Set the weekly behavioral goals with the patient and record on your Weekly Goal Completion Form for the next session. Have the patient write these in the space provided in the homework section of the corresponding workbook chapter.

✎ Ask patient to use the ABC Worksheet to identify the beliefs and consequences associated with three activating events this week. At least one of the events must be related to pain.

✎ Have patient work toward completing the weekly behavioral goals set at the end of the session.

Chapter 7

Session 5: Cognitive Restructuring

(Corresponds to chapter 6 of the workbook)

Materials Needed

- Weekly Goal Completion Form
- Restructuring Thoughts Worksheet

Outline

- Review homework
- Review the connection between negative thoughts and pain
- Teach cognitive restructuring
- Assign homework

Homework Review

Discuss any difficulties the patient had in completing the ABC worksheets and weekly behavioral goals. Take time to review the worksheets with the patient and correct any mistakes when distinguishing thoughts from emotions. Reinforce attempts at practice and problem-solve around failure to complete homework. Complete the Weekly Goal Completion Form for each homework assignment.

Briefly review the consequences of negative thoughts and specifically those thoughts related to pain. Even though negative thoughts in general are related to increased pain, pain-specific thoughts can make an even more significant contribution to the experience of pain as these thoughts can affect beliefs of self-efficacy and expectations of ability to cope with pain. Query the patient about his way of thinking about pain:

> *Can you think of a time when you have had any of these types of thoughts in response to pain?*
>
> ▩ *I can't cope with this.*
>
> ▩ *My pain is going to kill me.*
>
> ▩ *This pain is too much for me.*
>
> ▩ *I can't do a thing because of my pain.*
>
> ▩ *My pain is getting the better of me.*
>
> ▩ *I can't do anything right.*

Using the ABC model, what kinds of emotional consequences (feelings) do you experience when you have these kinds of thoughts? How does it make you feel or behave when you think in this way? How does it affect your pain?

Emphasize to the patient that it is the *thoughts* about an event, either positive or negative, that determine the emotions he will experience. In order to avoid unnecessary distress that affects his health and pain, he can learn to identify and change negative thoughts in favor of more positive thoughts.

Restructuring Thoughts

Next walk the patient through the cognitive restructuring procedure using the Restructuring Thoughts worksheet. Cognitive restructuring teaches patients to change negative emotions, along with the physical and behavioral consequences, by recognizing the maladaptive thoughts that give rise to the emotions and substituting more adaptive thoughts.

Follow these steps with the patient:

1. Ask the patient to think of a recent stressful situation that resulted in negative emotions and record this in the first column. (This can

be taken directly from one of the patient's ABC worksheets completed for last week's homework.)

2. Ask the patient to describe and record the emotions he was having at the time (e.g., anxious, frustrated, angry, sad, depressed) and rate the emotion from 0% to 100%.

3. Ask the patient to write down the thoughts (beliefs) he was having that led to the emotions. People often become confused between what constitutes a "thought" versus an "emotion," so you may need to spend some time describing the difference between the two.

4. Pay attention to the description of thoughts. While some of the patient's thoughts may be specifically related to the situation described, others may be more general automatic thoughts based on cognitive errors (e.g., "I never do anything right," "My life is miserable").

5. Evaluate the thoughts with the patient:
   ▪ Look for any evidence (facts) that the thought is true.
   ▪ Identify any evidence (facts) that the thought might not be true.

6. If there is evidence to suggest that the negative thought might not be entirely true, help the patient to write down a positive coping thought that is more consistent with the facts and evidence (e.g., "I'm learning some great skills to help me take control of my pain," "I don't have to let pain keep me from enjoying myself").

7. Ask the patient about the feelings he has when repeating the original negative thought compared to the positive coping thought. What emotion might have been felt if the patient had been thinking the positive coping thought in that situation? How would repeating the positive coping thought affect his physical reactions and his behaviors? Have the patient rate the emotion from 0% to 100%. Has the rating of the original emotion changed?

Continue practicing cognitive restructuring with the patient using the following examples (see figures 7.1 and 7.2) or examples from the patient's ABC sheet.

Situation	Emotion	Automatic Thought	Evidence for	Evidence against	Positive Coping Thought	Emotion
Describe the event that led to the unpleasant emotion.	Specify sad, angry, etc., and rate the emotion from 0% to 100%.	Write the automatic thought that preceded the emotion.	What is the evidence that this thought is true?	What is the evidence that this thought is false?	What else can I say to myself instead of the automatic thought?	Re-rate the emotion from 0% to 100%.
A pain flare-up on a busy day.	Depressed 60% Frustrated 50%	I can't cope with my pain; my life is miserable.	There is too much going on today. I feel overwhelmed and I'm not getting my work done.	I have had busy days before when I've been in pain and I was able to handle my pain and all my responsibilities well. I'm usually very productive. My life isn't all bad (I have a great family).	Not every day is this hectic and some days are good. I have made it through very hectic days before and I can do it again.	Depressed 25% Frustrated 30%

Note that while one of the thoughts is pain-specific, the patient has also brought in an automatic thought about life in general being miserable. With this cognitive error, he discounts the positive aspects of his life.

Figure 7.1

Example of Completed Restructuring Thoughts Worksheet for a Pain-Specific Situation

Situation	Emotion	Automatic Thought	Evidence for	Evidence against	Positive Coping Thought	Emotion
Describe the event that led to the unpleasant emotion.	Specify sad, angry, etc., and rate the emotion from 0% to 100%.	Write the automatic thought that preceded the emotion.	What is the evidence that this thought is true?	What is the evidence that this thought is false?	What else can I say to myself instead of the automatic thought?	Re-rate the emotion from 0% to 100%.
Stuck in line at the grocery store behind someone who is moving slowly.	Angry 50% Frustrated 70%	This always happens to me; I'm going to be here forever. People are so inconsiderate.	I was stuck behind a slow person last time I was here.	There have been times that I've gone through this line very quickly. I know I will not be here forever. The person is probably not doing it on purpose.	A 5-minute delay is not worth getting upset. I can kill a few minutes by reading the magazine covers; I would waste this much time at home anyway.	Angry 20% Frustrated 25%

Note that in this example the person has brought in an automatic thought about people in general being inconsiderate. This cognitive error serves to increase the intensity of the emotions in this situation.

Figure 7.2

Example of Completed Restructuring Thoughts Worksheet for a General Stressful Situation

Set the weekly behavioral goals with the patient and record on your Weekly Goal Completion Form for the next session. Have the patient write these in the space provided in the homework section of the corresponding workbook chapter.

✎ Ask patient to practice cognitive restructuring for three thoughts during the week using the Restructuring Thoughts Worksheet. One of the thoughts must be specific to pain.

✎ Have patient work toward completing the weekly behavioral goals set at the end of the session.

Chapter 8

Session 6: Stress Management

(Corresponds to chapter 7 of the workbook)

Materials Needed

- Weekly Goal Completion Form

Outline

- Review homework
- Define stress
- Explain the "fight-or-flight" response
- Review common sources of stress
- Discuss the relationship between stress and pain
- Examine ways to decrease stress
- Assign homework

Homework Review

Discuss any difficulties the patient had in completing the Restructuring Thoughts Worksheets and weekly behavioral goals. Take time to review the worksheets with the patient. Reinforce attempts at practice and problem-solve around failure to complete homework. Complete Weekly Goal Completion Form for each homework assignment.

Begin by providing a basic definition of stress. Use the "bell-shaped curve" diagram (Fig. 8.1) to explain the relationship between arousal and performance. The following dialogue can be used to begin the discussion on stress:

With every major event in our lives (a health problem, the birth of a child, or a new relationship), there are changes that require us to mobilize resources and make adjustments. Some events, such as deadlines, competitions, and confrontations, may produce feelings of eagerness and excitement, particularly when we think that we have a chance of succeeding. The arousal you feel when you try to meet these challenges is considered healthy.

However, when a situation or event is perceived by a person as being overwhelming, beyond her abilities to cope, and threatening to her well-being, it is considered "stressful." Stress can result in feelings of exhaustion, fatigue, and depression, which in turn can lead to health problems such as headaches, upset stomach, rashes, insomnia, ulcers,

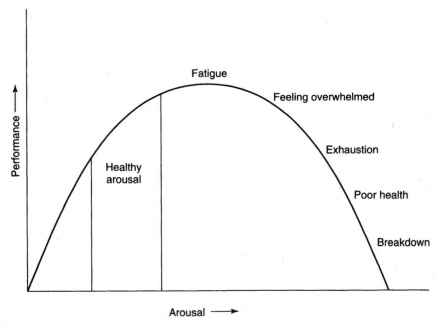

Figure 8.1
Arousal and Performance

high blood pressure, heart disease, and stroke. Stress can also affect work performance and relationships.

Ask the patient if she has noticed the difference between good stress and unhealthy stress in her own life. Emphasize that it is not the events themselves that cause stress, but how a person reacts to them. In the same situation, one person may feel a healthy amount of arousal, while another person may feel "stressed out."

The Fight-or-Flight Response

Explain to the patient that stress is related to a primitive system in our body called the "fight-or-flight" response. It is called this because it provides the strength and energy to either fight or run away from danger. The physical changes that occur when this system is activated include the following:

- An increase in heart rate and blood pressure (to get more blood to the muscles, brain, and heart)

- Faster breathing (to take in more oxygen)

- Tensing of muscles (to prepare for actions like running)

- Increased mental alertness and sensitivity of sense organs (to assess the situation and act quickly)

- Increased blood flow to the brain, heart, and muscles (the organs that are most important in dealing with danger)

- Less blood to the skin, digestive tract, kidneys, and liver (where it is least needed in times of crisis)

- An increase in blood sugar, fats, and cholesterol (for extra energy)

- A rise in platelets and blood clotting factors (to prevent hemorrhage in case of injury)

Although this system was adaptive in the past (e.g., to help our ancestors in hunting), it is not always appropriate today. In fact, when this system is turned on for long periods of time it can have harmful effects on the body (e.g., decreased immune function, heart disease).

Common Sources of Stress

Now that you have reviewed stress and its effects, help the patient recognize sources of stress in her life. See Table 8.1 and Table 8.2 for potential external and internal sources of stress. While reviewing these tables ask the patient if any of these are sources of stress for her.

Relationship Between Stress and Pain

Go over the relationship between stress and pain with the patient, emphasizing the ways that pain and stress reinforce each other.

Table 8.1 External Stressors

Type	Examples
Physical environment	Noise, bright lights, heat, confined spaces
Social	Rudeness, bossiness, or aggressiveness on the part of someone else
Organizational	Rules, regulations, "red tape," deadlines
Major life events	Death of a relative, lost job, promotion, new baby
Daily hassles	Commuting, misplacing keys, mechanical breakdowns

Table 8.2 Internal Stressors

Type	Examples
Lifestyle choices	Caffeine, lack of sleep, overloaded schedule, unhealthy diet
Negative self-talk	Pessimistic thinking, self-criticism, over-analyzing
Mind traps	Unrealistic expectations, taking things personally, all-or-nothing thinking, exaggerating, rigid thinking
Stressful personality traits	Perfectionist, workaholic, have to please others

Pain Leads to Stress

Based on the definition of stress given in the opening of this session, the sensations of pain and even all of the experiences associated with chronic pain (e.g., disability, job loss, marital problems) are considered stressful only if a person believes that the demands exceed her ability to cope with them. However, for many people with chronic pain, it is considered to be a significant source of stress in their lives.

Stress Leads to Pain

Stress is associated with perceptions of limited ability to cope, low self-efficacy, and poor problem-solving skills. These factors can contribute to depression and negative mood, which can increase pain. These may also result in decreased efforts to take personal responsibility for the management of pain. Such a person may be more prone to rely on others (e.g., physicians) to prescribe pain medication or perform some type of intervention to relieve her pain. Feeling a lack of control over pain can raise stress levels, which in turn can lead to increased pain.

Briefly discuss with the patient how stress and pain interact with one another in her own life. For example, ask her to recall a recent stressful event and to discuss how that event affected her pain level.

Ways to Decrease Stress

Given the relationship between stress and pain, it is important to be aware of sources of stress and ways to decrease stress. There are several kinds of changes a person can make to help manage stress:

Change Lifestyle Habits

- Decrease caffeine intake (coffee, tea, colas, chocolate)

- Maintain a well-balanced diet and decrease consumption of junk food

- Eat slowly and at regular intervals

- Exercise regularly (at least 30 minutes three times per week)

- Get adequate sleep (figure out how much you need)

- Take time-outs and leisure time (do something for yourself every day)

- Do relaxation exercises (e.g., breathing, imagery, PMR)

Discuss with the patient which of her lifestyle habits may need changing and problem-solve around difficulties in making changes.

Change How You Approach Situations

- Time and money management

- Assertiveness (see Chapter 11)

- Problem-solving coping skills

Inquire if the patient has difficulties in these areas. Work with the patient on how she can gain these skills.

Change Your Thinking

- Have realistic expectations (when expectations are more realistic, life seems more manageable)

- Keep a sense of humor (being able to see the humor in the things helps to lighten the situation)

- Have a support system (speak with someone or write down your thoughts)

- Focus on the positive (think half-full vs. half-empty)

- Challenge negative thinking using cognitive restructuring skills (see Chapter 7)

Ask the patient which of these ways of thinking she needs to improve on the most. Encourage her to rethink recent or upcoming situations using these strategies.

Set the weekly behavioral goals with the patient and record on your Weekly Goal Completion Form for the next session. Have the patient write these in the space provided in the homework section of the corresponding workbook chapter.

✎ Ask patient to identify external and internal stressors in her life. These can be recorded in the tables provided in the workbook.

✎ Have patient select changes she would like to try to make in order to decrease stress and record these on the My Life Changes form in the workbook.

✎ Have patient work toward completing the weekly behavioral goals set at the end of the session.

Chapter 9 | *Session 7: Time-Based Pacing*

(Corresponds to chapter 8 of the workbook)

Materials Needed

- Weekly Goal Completion Form
- Activity Pacing Worksheet

Outline

- Review homework
- Introduce time-based pacing
- Teach steps to appropriate pacing
- Discuss pacing techniques
- Assign homework

Homework Review

Discuss any difficulties the patient had in completing the homework and weekly behavioral goals. Reinforce attempts at practice and problem-solve around failure to complete homework. Complete the Weekly Goal Completion Form for each homework assignment.

When some people begin a project it is very hard for them to stop working on it before it's completed. They work on the project nonstop despite the onset of pain. As a result of "working through" the pain, the level of pain becomes higher and higher. This can sometimes result in severe pain that requires rest for an extended period, sometimes days, before being able to work again. Once the pain decreases, the person may feel he has to work extra hard in order to catch up on time lost. He does everything on his "to do" list on that day, only to end up in more pain for days afterwards. This cycle of work, pain, and rest is very common for individuals who have chronic pain (Fig. 9.1).

One method for breaking this cycle is called *time-based pacing*. Time-based pacing is a process in which activity breaks are based on time intervals, not on how much of the job is completed (Fig. 9.2).

You can use the following example to illustrate how it works:

> *For example, suppose you decide to paint your bedroom this weekend and you tell yourself that you don't want to overdo it so you're going to pace yourself by taking a break when half of the room is completed. Now imagine that the job takes longer than you thought, and by the time you are halfway finished with the room you have spent hours on your feet and you are in a lot of pain. If you had paced yourself by the amount of time spent active (e.g., breaks every 20 minutes before the pain starts) rather than the amount of the job completed, you might have been able to avoid the onset of pain.*

Some people are reluctant to pace themselves because they think they can't afford to "slow down." Explain to the patient that by taking breaks before pain begins (not after pain gets bad), he will be able to return to activity sooner and will actually get more done. By using *time* rather than *pain* as an indicator, he will not need long periods of rest to recover from pain because the pain flare-up will never happen. The following example may help convince patients of the value of pacing:

> *For example, professional athletes (e.g., basketball, hockey, football) take regular water breaks on the sidelines in order to perform at peak efficiency. Their coaches know that if players are kept in the game*

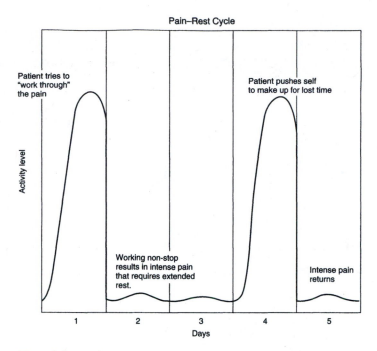

Figure 9.1

Pain–Rest Cycle Graph

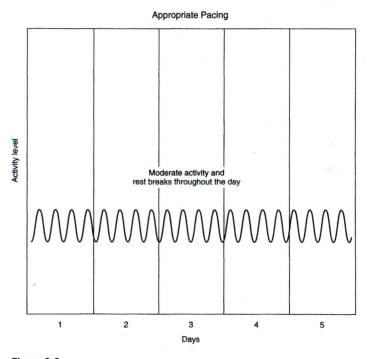

Figure 9.2

Time-Based Pacing Graph

until they are tired, then they will not be performing at their best. The same reasoning should apply to you.

Discuss with the patient whether he has difficulty pacing himself. Emphasize the consequences of not taking breaks and the increased productivity that comes with time-based pacing.

Steps to Time-Based Pacing

Identify with the patient a few activities on which he can try pacing in the coming week. Introduce the Activity Pacing Worksheet with the following steps. Figure 9.3 shows a completed example of the worksheet. A blank copy is included in the workbook.

1. *Identify a task that you typically do every day that increases your pain. Alternatively, is there something you are planning to do this week that you are concerned may cause you increased pain? Put this in the Activity column of the worksheet.*

2. *Estimate how long you can do the task safely without creating a pain flare-up; this will be your "active" time. The amount of time should be a few minutes less than the point when pain begins. Write your "active" time in the Goal column of the worksheet next to the activity.*

3. *Estimate how long you will need to rest before becoming active again in order to avoid pain flare-ups; this will be called your "rest" time. Write this in the Goal column of the worksheet next to the activity.*

4. *As you perform the activity, record your actual "active" and "rest" times for each day on the Activity Pacing Worksheet.*

If possible, do this for two other tasks that cause an increase in pain, remembering that different types of activities will require different activity/rest schedules. Remind the patient that estimates are not always accurate the first time, so he may need to adjust the schedule as he goes. If flare-ups do occur, he should cut the activity level in half at first and over three days build back up to the previous level of activity. Encourage the patient to expand the activity/rest schedule to other activities and slowly build up the active time. Emphasize that he should not stop practicing time-based pacing skills even when he is feeling good or pain-free. Pacing needs to be consistent in order to be an effective pain-reducing strategy.

Activity Pacing Worksheet

Activity	GOAL	Day 1	Day 2	Day 3	Day 4	Day 5	Day 6	Day 7
Walking	**Active:** 7 minutes **Resting:** 10 minutes	**Active:** 4 minutes **Resting:** 15 minutes	**Active:** 5 minutes **Resting:** 15 minutes	**Active:** 9 minutes **Resting:** 12 minutes	**Active:** 5 minutes **Resting:** 12 minutes	**Active:** 6 minutes **Resting:** 12 minutes	**Active:** 7 minutes **Resting:** 12 minutes	**Active:** 7 minutes **Resting:** 10 minutes
Working on the computer	**Active:** 20 minutes **Resting:** 10 minutes	**Active:** 15 minutes **Resting:** 11 minutes	**Active:** 22 minutes **Resting:** 17 minutes	**Active:** 15 minutes **Resting:** 15 minutes	**Active:** 19 minutes **Resting:** 30 minutes	**Active:** 10 minutes **Resting:** 10 minutes	**Active:** 21 minutes **Resting:** 11 minutes	**Active:** 20 minutes **Resting:** 12 minutes
Cleaning the house	**Active:** 30 minutes **Resting:** 30 minutes	**Active:** 25 minutes **Resting:** 26 minutes	**Active:** 27 minutes **Resting:** 37 minutes	**Active:** 35 minutes **Resting:** 29 minutes	**Active:** 30 minutes **Resting:** 40 minutes	**Active:** 28 minutes **Resting:** 25 minutes	**Active:** 30 minutes **Resting:** 26 minutes	**Active:** 35 minutes **Resting:** 29 minutes

Figure 9.3

Example of Completed Activity Pacing Worksheet

At the end of the session, review some general pacing techniques with the patient:

■ Maintain an awareness of your activities and how you do them.

■ Avoid rushing and crowded schedules of activities.

■ Plan: make a weekly calendar and spread activities evenly throughout the week.

■ Make a flexible daily schedule.

■ Prioritize activities.

■ Set reasonable goals for total activity.

■ Use time-contingent rather than pain-contingent termination of activities.

■ Use relaxation and other pain coping strategies.

Discuss the patient's current style of activity planning and pacing, and review any ways that the patient can improve his lifestyle by scheduling and pacing. Suggest the idea of incorporating mini-sessions of progressive muscle relaxation, deep breathing, or visual imagery into planned rest periods at work or at home.

Homework

Set the weekly behavioral goals with the patient and record on your Weekly Goal Completion Form for the next session. Have the patient write these in the space provided in the homework section of the corresponding workbook chapter.

✎ Have patient practice time-based pacing for several activities using the Activity Pacing Worksheet.

✎ Have patient work toward completing the weekly behavioral goals set at the end of the session.

Chapter 10 | *Session 8: Pleasant Activity Scheduling*

(Corresponds to chapter 9 of the workbook)

Materials Needed

- Weekly Goal Completion Form
- Pleasant Activities List
- Pleasant Activity Scheduling worksheet

Outline

- Review homework
- Identify pleasant activities
- Schedule pleasant activities
- Assign homework

Homework Review

Discuss any difficulties the patient had in completing the activity pacing homework and weekly behavioral goals. Reinforce attempts at practice and problem-solve around failure to complete homework. Complete the Weekly Goal Completion Form for each homework assignment.

Pleasant Activity Scheduling

The experience of pain can be associated with reduced activity or social withdrawal. These may be the result of physical limitations related to structural pathology or the patient's belief that she is physically disabled and unable to perform some activities without hurting herself. Alternatively, these may be self-imposed for reasons such as not wanting to answer questions about pain (e.g., "You don't look like you're in pain; what's wrong with you?"), feeling embarrassed, or feeling frustrated over limitations. Consequently, a patient may isolate herself and stop doing the things that she once found the most enjoyable. Once removed from reinforcing activities and positive social situations, it is likely that the patient will become depressed, which can contribute to disability and the experience of pain.

One way to help prevent this from happening is to plan an increased number of pleasant activities throughout the week. The introduction of more positive activities into the patient's life may help to reduce negative thoughts and emotions, increase overall activity levels, and decrease pain. The first step is to identify things that the patient would like to start doing. The second step is to help her to schedule these activities into the week.

Choosing Pleasant Activities

Identifying enjoyable activities can sometimes be more difficult than anticipated, particularly if the patient has had pain for a long time and is not in the habit of doing enjoyable things for herself. Other times, a patient may identify activities that she would *like* to do but is not *able* to do because of structural pathology related to pain, or due to changes associated with normal aging. For example, an elderly gentleman with a back and shoulder injury may comment that he would like to be able to join a bowling team, bench press 200 pounds, or play 18 holes of golf when he has not done any of these activities since his 20s. Work with the patient to set achievable and realistic goals. While individuals may not always be able to perform the activities that they could when they were younger, there are often alternative ways of being involved in activities. For example, the patient may not be able to play 18 holes of golf, but he can probably putt on the putting green; another patient may not be able to make a three-course meal, but she can teach someone else to cook.

The activities can be things that patients have done in the recent past and would like to do again, things they have not done for some time, things they have never done but have always meant to do, or activities they would like to perform on a more frequent basis. If the patient is having trouble coming up with possible activities, review the Pleasant Activities List for ideas. Develop and adapt ideas as needed. Discuss how to pace pleasant activities that may be physically challenging.

Pleasant Activities List

1. Having a hobby
2. Relaxing
3. Exercising
4. Reading
5. Sightseeing
6. Listening to music
7. Spending time with friends
8. Playing or watching sports
9. Cleaning
10. Going on a date
11. Traveling
12. Cooking
13. Thinking positive thoughts
14. Dancing
15. Enjoying nature
16. Playing games
17. Eating
18. Repairing things
19. Having family gatherings
20. Writing
21. Playing music
22. Going to a play or lecture
23. Learning something new
24. Taking care of yourself
25. Shopping
26. Telling jokes
27. Playing with animals
28. Taking a class
29. Pampering yourself
30. Going to a museum
31. Talking on the phone
32. Entertaining
33. Collecting things
34. Going for a walk
35. Thinking about good memories
36. Watching children play
37. Singing
38. Organizing
39. Going to a party or event
40. Planning for the future
41. Joining a club
42. Dressing up
43. Daydreaming
44. Taking or looking at pictures
45. Doing arts and crafts
46. Teaching
47. Solving a problem, puzzle, or crossword
48. Volunteering
49. Practicing religion
50. Having a discussion

One way to increase the likelihood that the patient will perform the activity is to work with her to schedule it into her week. Otherwise, the patient could procrastinate and end up not performing the activity before the next session. For example, if a patient identified reading a new book as a pleasant activity, you could discuss details with the patient such as the kind of book she wants to read and where she would find it, the time of day and the day of the week she would have time to read, or any barriers to setting aside time to read. Procrastination and avoidance can get in the way of completing homework, even when the homework is something fun.

Have the patient use the Pleasant Activity Schedule worksheet in the workbook to keep track of her pleasant activities for the week. This will help her keep her commitment to doing the chosen activities and feel a sense of accomplishment for completing activities.

Homework

Set the weekly behavioral goals with the patient and record on your Weekly Goal Completion Form for the next session. Have the patient write these in the space provided in the homework section of the corresponding workbook chapter.

✎ Ask patient to schedule at least two pleasant activities for the week using the Pleasant Activity Schedule worksheet.

✎ Have patient work toward completing the weekly behavioral goals set at the end of the session.

✎ Remind patient about the importance of pacing, even when something is enjoyable.

Chapter 11 | *Session 9: Anger Management*

(Corresponds to chapter 10 of the workbook)

Materials Needed

- Weekly Goal Completion Form
- Restructuring Thoughts Worksheet

Outline

- Review homework
- Define anger
- Discuss the relationship between anger and pain
- Teach anger management
- Discuss response styles and introduce assertive responding
- Assign homework

Homework Review

Discuss any difficulties the patient had in completing the pleasant activity scheduling homework and weekly behavioral goals. Reinforce attempts at practice and problem-solve around failure to complete homework. Complete the Weekly Goal Completion Form for each homework assignment.

What Is Anger?

Explain that anger is a natural emotional response that we all have from time to time. It is an emotion that can range from mild irritation to intense rage. The experience of anger is related to the way we think about something that happens. Anger can produce physical changes in the body such as increased heart rate and blood pressure and the release of adrenaline (recall the "fight-or-flight" response discussed in Chapter 8). We can actually feel some of these changes, like tense muscles and a flushed face, as they occur. When we are feeling threatened, anger is an adaptive response because it prepares us to attack or defend ourselves. Anger can also result in behavior changes such as yelling, threatening posturing, or attacking.

Tell the patient that though anger is a natural reaction, it is important to keep it under control. When anger is allowed to go unchecked it can actually begin to fuel itself and cause more anger. It's hard to think clearly when angry, and people who are angry often say things they normally wouldn't, which can lead to regrets once the anger has subsided and calmer thoughts are in control. In addition, prolonged anger can be a psychological stressor and can have a negative impact on the body, including the experience of pain. Figure 11.1 may be helpful in describing the chain reaction of anger to the patient.

Anger and Pain

People who have chronic pain often say that their pain seems worse when they get really angry. There may be several reasons for this. First, anger

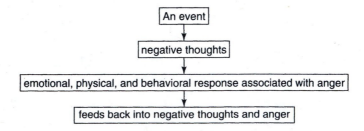

Figure 11.1
Anger Chain Reaction

is often associated with increased muscle tension, which may cause an increase in pain, particularly if the muscle tension is in an area affected by pain. Second, when people experience negative thoughts and emotions related to one situation, it may lead them to focus on all things negative in their lives, and this can include pain and its associated problems. In terms of the gate control theory discussed earlier, anger may result in an opening of the pain gate, allowing more information about pain to reach the brain. It is also the case that pain lowers the anger threshold for some people, such that minor irritations and stressors become magnified and trigger feelings of anger. The following questions may help engage the patient in the discussion:

- *When in pain, do you find yourself more likely to become irritated or angry?*

- *When angry, do you feel your pain increasing?*

Anger Management

Now that you have discussed anger and its relationship with pain, the next goal is to teach your patient ways to keep anger under control. There are three important steps to review with the patient: develop awareness; modify internal responses; and respond assertively.

Step 1: Develop Awareness

Environmental Awareness

Be aware of triggers for anger in your environment, including:
- *Verbal/physical abuse or sarcasm (e.g., is there a person who knows just what to say to make you angry?)*
- *Annoyances and irritations (e.g., excessive noise, interruptions, or minor accidents)*
- *Common frustrations (e.g., you are prevented, blocked, or disappointed)*
- *Perceived injustices (e.g., you feel you have been treated unfairly)*

Physical Awareness

Be aware of physical changes in your body that can serve as warning signs that you are becoming angry, such as heart racing, muscle tension, making a fist, jaw clenching, face turning red or warm.

Behavioral Awareness

Be aware of behavioral changes, such as pacing back and forth or stiff posture. How we behave when we get angry can determine whether anger will fade or continue to get worse.

Discuss each of these points with your patient, asking if he is aware of any specific triggers for anger, physical warning signs of anger, or behaviors when he starts getting mad.

Now that the patient understands how to become aware of the onset of anger, the next step is to develop strategies for coping with the feelings of anger once they arise. Emphasize that it is important to put a stop to anger before it gets too far out of control.

Step 2: Modify Internal Responses

Physical

Use relaxation skills like diaphragmatic breathing, progressive muscle relaxation, or imagery when you feel yourself becoming angry. These techniques are helpful to counter the physical changes (e.g., increased heart rate, tense muscles) that occur when you become angry. Try all of these techniques and use the one that works best for you.

Cognitive

■ *Try to consider the feelings of others. Anger often occurs because we assume that we know what other people are thinking and feeling. In reality, we do not: no one can read minds or predict the future.*

- *Think about your own feelings. Are you really angry about this, or is it something else?*

- *Use humor to take the edge off anger or to defuse the situation.*

- *Use cognitive restructuring techniques:*
  1. *Identify the automatic thoughts behind the feelings of anger (e.g., "she did that on purpose," "he has always hated me," or "she doesn't care about me").*
  2. *Avoid traps that increase your anger (e.g., believing that everyone is out to get you, thinking that you must have everything your way, exaggerating the importance of an event). This is important because internal conversations can fuel anger and prolong it long after the incident has occurred.*
  3. *Challenge cognitive errors/negative thoughts and generate alternative interpretations of events.*
  4. *Replace unhelpful negative thoughts with more positive coping thoughts.*

Step 3: Respond Assertively

The third step to anger management is to learn constructive ways to take action or express an opinion. First, however, it is helpful to review with the patient two common response styles that are less adaptive.

Less Adaptive Response Styles

Withdrawal and Avoidance

A person who responds in this way avoids dealing with conflict or angry emotions. The issue that caused the anger is left unresolved and the negative emotions are left ready to resurface at another time. Avoidance can even cause the anger to grow and create resentment toward others, as a person may continue to think about the event after it has passed (e.g., internal conversations about how he should have responded).

Aggression, Antagonism, and Hostility

A person who responds in this way becomes aggressive or threatening when angry. This type of response can lead others to feel guarded or edgy, or it may elicit hostility since the other person feels he is being attacked. This kind of person may not get pushed around very often, but no one will want to be around him.

Assertive Responding

Explain to the patient that this is the most adaptive way of responding when you are feeling angry. Assertive behavior means standing up for your rights and expressing what you believe, feel, and want in a direct, honest, and appropriate way that respects the rights of others. The advantage of being assertive is that you can often get what you want, usually without making others angry. If you are assertive, you can act in your own best interest and not feel guilty or wrong about it. An assertive person can express his likes and interests spontaneously, can talk about himself without being self-conscious, can accept compliments comfortably, can disagree with someone openly, can ask for clarification, and can say "no." In short, when you are an assertive person, you can be more relaxed in interpersonal situations.

How to Respond Assertively

■ *Confront the person you are angry with at an appropriate time and place. Wait until your emotions are under control so that you can communicate more effectively.*

■ *Communicate a willingness to understand the other person's point of view. It's important to be respectful of other people's opinions.*

■ *Using "I" statements, be direct and tell the person why you are angry and what exactly led to your becoming angry. Example of an "I" statement: "I feel angry when you spend a lot of money without talking to me about it first."*

Emphasize to the patient that being assertive is not always easy, but it is important for effective communication with others and can help to reduce tension and anger.

Guidelines for Communicating with Others Assertively

1. Maintain eye contact and position your body squarely toward others. Look the other person in the eye most of the time but do not stare fixedly. Lean forward and use hand gestures to maintain his attention.

2. Speak firmly and positively, and loudly enough to be heard easily. Avoid mumbling, whining, speaking shrilly, or yelling. Avoid dropping your voice at the end of a sentence.

3. Use clear, concise speech. Ask directly for what you want, or say clearly what you don't want. Avoid numerous repetitions and qualifiers such as "maybe" or "I guess." Avoid undoing statements such as "I shouldn't ask, but . . ."

4. Make sure your nonverbal behavior matches the content of your statement. Don't smile when refusing or disagreeing. Don't wring your hands when requesting. Avoid a rigid face when expressing warmth or praise.

5. Listen. Repeat the point that the other person made, clarify, or say something that shows that you are listening.

6. Maintain a posture and attitude of equality. Avoid apologetic statements or a tone that belittles yourself or your ideas. Avoid accusing statements or a tone of sarcasm or ridicule. Be respectful of yourself and others.

7. Take the initiative. Don't let others choose for you. Take the lead with "I have a suggestion . . ." or "In my opinion . . ."

Set the weekly behavioral goals with the patient and record on your Weekly Goal Completion Form for the next session. Have the patient write these in the space provided in the homework section of the corresponding workbook chapter.

✎ Ask patient to complete the Restructuring Thoughts worksheet (see Session 5) for events that led to feelings of anger.

✎ Have patient work toward completing the weekly behavioral goals set at the end of the session.

Chapter 12 | *Session 10: Sleep Hygiene*

(Corresponds to chapter 11 of the workbook)

Materials Needed

- Weekly Goal Completion Form

Outline

- Review homework
- Explain the necessity of sleep
- Discuss ways to improve sleep
- Assign homework

Homework Review

Discuss any difficulties the patient had in completing the anger management homework and weekly behavioral goals. Reinforce attempts at practice and problem-solve around failure to complete homework. Complete the Weekly Goal Completion Form for each homework assignment.

Begin by asking the patient about her sleep and if sleep has been an issue for her in the past. Although there are many types of sleep problems that a person may have, common problems for people who have pain include difficulty falling asleep and problems staying asleep due to pain. Even if sleep has not been an issue for the patient, a review of good sleep habits can be beneficial.

Explain to the patient that sleep is an opportunity for our bodies to repair themselves, both physically (e.g., torn muscles, organ cleansing) and psychologically (e.g., working through anxiety). Each sleep cycle (which lasts about 100 minutes) is divided into physically repairing sleep and psychologically repairing sleep. When we first fall asleep, more time is spent in physically repairing sleep; later in the sleep cycle, more time is spent in psychologically repairing sleep. Age influences the balance between these two types of sleep. Babies spend more time in psychologically repairing sleep (dream state) because their bodies don't need much physical repair. Older adults spend more time in physically repairing sleep because their bodies are more vulnerable to damage.

When factors such as physiological hyperarousal (anxiety), affective distress and worry (depression), or poor sleep habits interfere with sleep patterns, the natural ability of the body to repair itself becomes disrupted. If disrupted for an extended period of time, needed physiological repair cannot take place, which can lead to increased fatigue and pain.

Review with the patient some of the other effects of not getting a good night's sleep:

- Increased emotional distress and irritability

- Increased clumsiness and poor coordination

- Decreased work performance and memory lapses

- Increased risk of automobile accidents

- Difficulty concentrating

While there are a number of sleep medications available on the market today, almost all of them have significant side effects, and none is meant to be used as a long-term solution to sleep problems. In this next section you will review ways the patient can improve sleep simply by changing some of her nighttime routines. These strategies fall under several categories.

Timing

■ *Establish a pattern to your sleep by going to bed at the same time each evening and getting out of bed at the same time every day, even on weekends, regardless of how much you have slept.*

■ *Avoid taking naps, but if you do nap make it no more than about 25 minutes. If you have problems falling asleep at night, then you should not take naps.*

Sleep Behavior

■ *Establish a pre-sleep ritual to give your body cues that it is time to slow down (e.g., taking a bath or reading for a few minutes before bed).*

■ *Use the bed only for sleep or for sex. Do not use your bed as a desk; do not read, eat, or watch TV in bed.*

■ *If you are unable to sleep for more than 15 minutes, then get out of bed. Lying in bed and feeling frustrated will not help. Engage in a quiet, nonstimulating activity and return to bed when you are sleepy.*

■ *Restrict the amount of time you spend in bed to your usual amount of sleep (e.g., 7 hours) even if you have not slept as well as you would have liked.*

Environment Tips

■ *Sleeping is associated with a decline in core body temperature from a state of relative warmth. You can raise your body temperature by taking a warm bath 20 minutes before bed.*

- *Fluctuations in room temperature disrupt the dream state, so maintain a steady temperature in the room throughout the night. A cool room is more conducive to sleep than a warm room.*

- *Eliminate illuminated wall clocks or other sources of light. (Note: An exception is a night light, which is often needed to avoid falling when getting up during the night.)*

Ingestion

- *Avoid caffeine (a stimulant) four to six hours before bedtime.*

- *Avoid nicotine (a stimulant) near bedtime and when waking at night.*

- *Beware of alcohol use. Though alcohol (a depressant) may initially promote sleep onset, it causes awakenings later in the night.*

- *If hungry before bed, have a light snack, which may be sleep-inducing. Eating a heavy meal too close to bedtime, however, might interfere with sleep.*

Mental Control

- *Avoid mentally stimulating activity just before going to bed (e.g., action movies, stimulating conversation, loud music).*

- *Try relaxation techniques such as deep breathing and visual imagery. Relaxation can help you get to sleep.*

- *Do mentally quiet tasks such as listening to relaxing music, thinking calming thoughts, and so forth. These can help you get to sleep.*

Discuss with the patient which of these strategies might be of use to her. You can work with the patient to implement the strategy—for example, help her come up with a suitable pre-sleep ritual or snack.

Set the weekly behavioral goals with the patient and record on your Weekly Goal Completion Form for the next session. Have the patient write these in the space provided in the homework section of the corresponding workbook chapter.

✎ Ask patient to use the Sleep Hygiene Worksheet in the workbook to log sleep habits and strategies over the next week.

✎ Ask patient to identify the assignments that she has found to be the most effective throughout the program.

✎ Have patient work toward completing the weekly behavioral goals set at the end of the session.

Chapter 13 | *Session 11: Relapse Prevention and Flare-Up Planning*

(Corresponds to chapter 12 of the workbook)

Materials Needed

- Weekly Goal Completion Form

Outline

- Review homework
- Discuss relapse prevention and flare-up planning
- Present stages of flare-up management
- Review patient's progress
- Terminate therapy

Homework Review

Discuss any difficulties the patient had in completing the sleep hygiene homework and weekly behavioral goals. Reinforce attempts at practice and problem-solve around failure to complete homework. Complete the Weekly Goal Completion Form for each homework assignment.

Relapse Prevention and Flare-Up Planning

Although your patient has certainly learned some effective skills for managing chronic pain, it is unlikely that his pain has been completely eliminated. In fact, it is more likely that he will have a "flare-up" or tem-

Table 13.1 Typical Components of a Pain Flare-Up

Pain Sensation	Automatic Thoughts	Mood Shift	Result
Marked increase or flare-up in pain sensation	*Expectation:* "I thought I learned ways to decrease my pain." *Loss of control:* "I can't deal with this." *Catastrophizing:* "This is unbearable."	Mood becomes negative (e.g., anxiety, depression)	Decrease in activity

porary increase of pain in the future. The patient probably already knows this and may have already had a period of increased pain while in therapy with you. Emphasize to the patient that when a flare-up occurs, it does not mean that his participation in this program was all for nothing. Your patient needs to be prepared for a pain flare-up so that he doesn't abandon everything he has learned when it occurs.

For some patients, the first thing that comes to mind when a pain flare-up occurs is to take an extra dose of pain medication as prescribed by a physician. There are times when this approach may be appropriate; however, after completing this program patients are also armed with a variety of new skills they can use to help manage their pain. What they need now is a plan for how to use these skills when the pain returns. Table 13.1 lists the components of a flare-up.

How to Manage a Flare-Up

Review the steps for self-management of flare-ups and ask the patient if this approach makes sense. Have the patient give an example of a flare-up and apply the following flare-up planning stages.

Stage 1: Preparation

■ Prepare for a pain flare-up before it occurs.

■ Become aware of emotional and physical cues that pain is increasing.

- Rehearse positive statements regarding the ability to cope with pain; reject a helpless attitude.

- Stop negative thoughts and redirect attention to positive coping statements.

Stage 2: Confrontation

- Confront the pain flare-up by using the self-management strategies learned in this program.

- Switch strategies as necessary (e.g., imagery, diaphragmatic breathing, and cognitive restructuring).

Stage 3: Critical Moments

- Do not magnify the sensations. Negative thoughts only make the pain seem worse.

- Use positive coping statements in place of negative thoughts (e.g., "I've handled this much pain before, and I can do it again;" "I won't attempt to totally eliminate the pain, I'll just try to keep it manageable").

Emphasize to the patient that not giving way to negative thinking is key to managing a pain flare-up. By practicing the strategies learned in this program, he can prevent many negative thoughts from happening. If negative thoughts do occur, he can deliberately stop them. Ask him to recall the exercises on identifying cognitive errors and restructuring negative thoughts from Sessions 4 and 5. He now has the skills to replace the negative thoughts associated with the flare-up with positive coping statements and regain control. Here are some examples:

THOUGHT: "Things are going pretty badly. I can't take it anymore."

ALTERNATE THOUGHT: "This has happened before, and I know I can get through it. I have planned for this. I'll review the strategies I have put together for dealing with a flare-up and do my best to manage my pain."

THOUGHT: "My pain feels terrible. Things are falling apart just when I thought I was doing well. There is nothing I can do to help myself."

ALTERNATE THOUGHT: "I have the ability to manage my pain by using some of the skills I learned in the pain program. I might not be able to get rid of the pain completely, but I can bring it down a bit. Just take a slow deep breath."

Stage 4: Reflection and Planning

After the flare-up, the patient should positively reinforce himself for using the new strategies and reflect on how it went. By reviewing his efforts and picking out the strategies that worked the best, he can create a plan for how to manage the flare-up next time. For example, the patient may think to himself:

1. "I feel great about how I handled that pain flare-up. Even though it was about as bad as it gets for me, I didn't let negative thoughts get the better of me. Using positive coping statements really helped; I'll do that again next time."

2. "This time I let the pain go too far before I used one of my strategies to cope. Next time I'll catch it earlier and try diaphragmatic breathing at the first sign of pain."

3. "I think I'll make a list of everything that seems to work for me so that I can have it with me as a reminder when my pain starts to flare up next time."

Progress Review

Coping Strategies

Review the skills learned during treatment and discuss preferences the patient may have for particular sessions or techniques (e.g., breathing, PMR, imagery, restructuring thoughts).

Treatment Goals

1. Review the overall treatment goals set at the beginning of therapy and the patient's success with the weekly behavioral goals (see Weekly Goal Completion Forms). Discuss any barriers to completing goals and help the patient identify goals that need continued work. Any change in the right direction should be positively reinforced.

2. Briefly review individual homework assignments and positively reinforce the patient's attempts to complete homework. Acknowledge the patient's efforts to gain new skills and any progress in using the skills to cope with pain.

Future Plans and Objectives

1. Remind the patient that he should still be working toward unmet behavioral goals after the termination of treatment. Help the patient break down vague or large objectives into smaller steps and short-term goals.

2. Provide the patient with post-treatment assessment materials to be completed at the end of the session. These materials are typically identical to those completed by the patient during the initial pain assessment.

3. Make any necessary referrals for patient care.

Therapy Termination

Like any relationship that ends, therapy termination may be difficult for some patients. It's important to take sufficient time in the session to openly address how the patient is feeling about ending treatment. For example, some patients may feel that they are losing a source of support or will miss the opportunity to have such exclusive attention paid to their issues. Normalize these feelings and reassure the patient that he is ready to end treatment with you.

Reinforce to the patient that he has learned many skills while in therapy and will continue to benefit from this program long after it has ended. Leave your patient with a feeling of hope and encouragement that he is now able to be his own coach. Finally, congratulate the patient for completing the pain management program and for making the commitment to learning skills to help him take greater control of his pain.

Appendix *Pain Interview*

Pain Interview

Patient Name: _____

Age: _____

Evaluation Date: _____

Pain Location

Primary pain site: _____

Secondary pain site: _____

Details of Injury/Onset: _____

_____

_____

_____

_____

Date of Onset

Primary pain site: _____

Secondary pain site: _____

Descriptors (e.g., burning, electric, sharp): _____

_____

_____

_____

_____

Pain Rating (Scale: 0 = no pain; 10 = worst pain imaginable)

Current: _____

Within the past 2 weeks: Average _____;   Worst _____;   Least _____

Intermittent _____;   Constant _____

Pain Medications and Effectiveness: _____

_____

_____

_____

_____

Previous Treatments (What things have you tried?)

Physical Therapy: _____

Chiropractic: _____

Surgery: _____

Psychology: _____

Other: _____

Temporal Cycles (Have you noticed any patterns to the pain?): _____

_____

_____

_____

_____

Pain Triggers (What makes your pain increase?): _____

_____

_____

_____

_____

Pain Reducers (What makes your pain decrease?): _____

_____

_____

_____

_____

Coping Strategies (How do you cope with pain?): _____

_____

_____

_____

_____

Litigation pending?   Yes _____;   No _____

Personal Goals (What are your goals for treatment?): _____

_____

_____

_____

_____

Psychosocial History

Childhood (Where did you grow up? Who did you live with?): _____

_____

_____

_____

_____

Education: _____

_____

_____

_____

_____

_____

Past/Present Occupation: _____

_____

_____

_____

_____

Marital/Family Relationship: _____

_____

_____

_____

Living Situation (Where do you live? With whom? How do they respond to you when you're in pain?):

_____

_____

_____

_____

Recreational Activities: _____

_____

_____

_____

Typical Day (Describe a typical day for you): _____

_____

_____

_____

Impact of Pain (How has pain impacted your life?): _____

_____

_____

_____

_____

Substance Use

Past and Present Alcohol and/or Cigarette Use: _____

_____

_____

_____

Past and Present Recreational Drug Use: _____

_____

_____

_____

Affective Status

Prominent Mood Disorders (Based on DSM-IV Criteria) (Have you noticed any changes in your mood? Have you been feeling depressed? Have you experienced any anxiety?):

_____

_____

_____

Past or Present Participation in Individual or Group Therapy: _____

_____

_____

_____

Past/Present Psychiatric Hospitalizations: _____

_____

_____

_____

Psychopharmacological Medications: _____

_____

_____

_____

Goal Setting Worksheet

Goal	Some Improvement	Moderate Improvement	Maximum Improvement
1.			
2.			
3.			
4.			
5.			

References

Anderson, G. B. J. (1997). The epidemiology of spinal disorders. In J. W. Frymoyer (Ed.), *The Adult Spine; Principles and Practices* (2nd ed., pp. 93–141). New York: Raven Press.

Baumstark, K. E., & Buckelew, S. P. (1992). Fibromyalgia: Clinical signs, research findings, treatment implications, and future directions. *Annals of Behavioral Medicine, 14,* 282–291.

Beck, A. T., Steer, R. A., & Garbin, M. G. (1988). Psychometric properties of the Beck Depression Inventory: Twenty-five years of evaluation. *Clinical Psychology Review, 8,* 77–100.

Burns, D. D. (1999). *The Feeling Good Handbook* (Rev. ed.). New York: Plume/Penguin Books.

Byrne, Z. S., & Hochwarter, W. A. (2006). I get by with a little help from my friends: the interaction of chronic pain and organizational support and performance. *Journal of Occupational Health Psychology, 11*(3), 215–227.

Centers for Disease Control and Prevention, National Center for Health Statistics. *Health, United States, 2006, With Chartbook on Trends in the Health of Americans.* Hyattsville, MD: U. S. Government Printing Office.

Compas, B. E., Haaga, D. A., Keefe, F. J., Leitenberg, H., & Williams, D. A. (1998). Sampling of empirically supported psychological treatments from health psychology: smoking, chronic pain, cancer, and bulimia nervosa. *Journal of Consulting and Clinical Psychology, 66*(1), 89–112.

Eccleston, C., Morley, S., Williams, A., Yoke, L., & Mastroyannopoulou, K. (2002). Systematic review of randomized controlled trials of psychological therapy for chronic pain in children and adolescents, with a subset meta-analysis of pain relief. *Pain, 99,* 157–165.

Gureje, O., Von Korff, M., Simon, G. E., & Gater, R. (1998). Persistent pain and well-being. A World Health Organization study in primary care. *Journal of the American Medical Association, 280,* 147–151.

Hoffman, B. M., Papas, R. K., Chatkoff, D. K., & Kerns, R. D. (2007). Meta-analysis of psychological interventions for chronic low back pain. *Health Psychology, 26,* 1–9.

International Association for the Study of Pain (IASP). (1994). IASP Task Force on Taxonomy (pp. 209–214). H. Merskey, & N. Bogduk, (Eds.), IASP Press, Seattle.

Jensen, M. P., Turner, J. A., Romano, J. M., & Fisher, L. D. (1999). Comparative reliability and validity of chronic pain intensity measures. *Pain, 83,* 157–162.

Keefe, F. J., Crisson, J., Urban, B. J., & Williams, D. A. (1990). Analyzing chronic low back pain: The relative contribution of pain coping strategies. *Pain, 40,* 293–301.

Kerns, R. D., Turk, D. C., & Rudy, T. E. (1985). West Haven-Yale Multidimensional Pain Inventory (WHYMPI). *Pain, 23,* 345–356.

Lipon, R. B., Stewart, W. F., Diamond, S., Diamond, M. L., & Reed, M. (2001). Prevalence and burden of migraine in the United States: Data from the American Migraine Study II. *Headache, 41,* 646–657.

Max, M. B. (2003). How to move pain research from the margin to the mainstream. *Journal of Pain, 4*(7): 355–360.

McCracken, L. M., Zayfert, C., & Gross, R. T. (1997). The Pain Anxiety Symptoms Scale: Development and validation of a scale to measure fear of pain. *Pain, 50,* 67–73.

Melzack, R. (1975). McGill Pain Questionnaire: Major properties and scoring methods. *Pain, 1,* 277–299.

Melzack, R., & Wall, P.D. (1965). Pain mechanisms: A new theory. *Science, 50,* 971–979.

Merskey, H., & Bogduk, N. (Eds.) (1994). *Classification of Chronic Pain. IASP Task Force on Taxonomy* (pp. 209–214). Seattle: IASP Press.

Morley, S., Eccleston, C., & Williams, A. (1999). Systematic review and meta-analysis of randomized controlled trials of cognitive-behaviour therapy for chronic pain in adults, excluding headache. *Pain, 80,* 1–13.

Otis, J. D., Reid, M. C., & Kerns, R. D. (2005). The management of chronic pain in the primary care setting. In L. C. James & R. A. Folen (Eds.), *Primary Care Clinical Health Psychology: A Model for the Next Frontier.* Washington, D.C.: American Psychological Association Press.

Rasmussen, B. K., Jensen, R., Schroll, M., & Olsen, J. (1991). Epidemiology of headache in a general population—a prevalence study. *Journal of Clinical Epidemiology, 44,* 1147–1157.

Reading, A. E., Everitt, B. S., & Sledmere, C. M. (1982). The McGill Pain Questionnaire: A replication of its construction. *British Journal of Clinical Psychology, 21,* 339–349.

Riley, J., Robinson, M. E., & Geisser, M. E. (1999). Empirical subgroups of the Coping Strategies Questionnaire-Revised: A multisample study. *Clinical Journal of Pain, 15*(2), 111–116.

Spielberger, C., Gorsuch, R., & Luschene, N. (1976). *Manual for the State-Trait Anxiety Inventory.* Palo Alto, CA: Consulting Psychologists Press.

Sullivan, M., Bishop, S., & Pivik, J. (1995). The Pain Catastrophizing Scale: Development and Validation. *Psychological Assessment, 7*(4), 524–532.

Turner, J. A., Mancl, L., & Aaron, L. A. (2006). Short- and long-term efficacy of brief cognitive-behavioral therapy for patients with chronic temporomandibular disorder pain: A randomized, controlled trial. *Pain, 121,* 181–194.

Xuemei, R., Pietrobon, Sun, S., Liu, G., & Hey, L. (2004). Estimates and patterns of direct healthcare expenditures among individuals with back pain in the U.S. *Spine, 29*(1), 79–86.

About the Author

Dr. John D. Otis is an Associate Professor of Psychology and Psychiatry at Boston University. He is the Director of Medical Psychology at Boston University School of Medicine and the Director of Pain Management Psychology Services at the VA Boston Healthcare System. He received his PhD in Clinical Psychology from the University of Florida, specializing in the assessment and treatment of chronic pain. He currently has several funded research projects, including a research study investigating the efficacy of CBT for patients with painful diabetic neuropathy and a grant investigating the development of an integrated treatment for patients with comorbid chronic pain and posttraumatic stress disorder. Dr. Otis has published numerous scholarly articles and book chapters about pain throughout the lifespan, with a focus on the development of innovative approaches to pain management tailored to specialized patient populations.